Clyde Parker:
Pastor; University Professor; Businessman

Clyde Parker:
Pastor; University Professor; Businessman

All At Same Time: Orchestrated by God

Ernstena Phillips Parker Wood

Xulon Elite

Xulon Press Elite
2301 Lucien Way #415
Maitland, FL 32751
407.339.4217
www.xulonpress.com

Exulon Elite

© 2022 by Ernstena Phillips Parker Wood

All rights reserved solely by the author. The author guarantees all contents are original and do not infringe upon the legal rights of any other person or work. No part of this book may be reproduced in any form without the permission of the author.

Due to the changing nature of the Internet, if there are any web addresses, links, or URLs included in this manuscript, these may have been altered and may no longer be accessible. The views and opinions shared in this book belong solely to the author and do not necessarily reflect those of the publisher. The publisher therefore disclaims responsibility for the views or opinions expressed within the work.

Unless otherwise indicated, Scripture quotations taken from the Holy Bible, New International Version (NIV). Copyright © 1973, 1978, 1984, 2011 by Biblica, Inc.™. Used by permission. All rights reserved.

Paperback ISBN-13: 978-1-66286-396-7
Ebook ISBN-13: 978-1-66286-397-4

Table of Contents

Endorsements vii
Foreword xiii
Preface xv
Introduction xvii

1) We Were Born In North Carolina "Mill" Towns 1
2) Living Conditions On a Farm In The 1900s. 3
3) The Phillips, Parker and Glover Families Meet 7
4) Gold Hill Christian School In The 1920s 9
5) The Roy Phillips Family Keeps Moving 11
6) Living in Kannapolis, The Cannon Family's Mill Town 13
7) Clyde's Musical Abilities Grow 15
8) Driver's License At Fifteen 17
9) College Plans Almost Torpedoed 19
10) Clyde's Busy Mid-Teens 21
11) Married At Eighteen 23
12) Clyde's First Pastorate at Nineteen 25
13) Back Home In North Carolina 27
14) Parker's Motel in Kannapolis 31
15) Clyde's Adventurous Children 35
16) More Elkin Memories 39
17) Color Blind 47
18) Clyde's Third Track–Business Man 49

19) Clyde's Overseas Travels 53
20) Tough–But Happy Times. 57
21) Two Years as President of Kernersville Pilgrim
    Bible College 61
22) Plant "Prayer Seeds" Early In Life. 63
23) From Elkin To High Point First Wesleyan Church 65
24) More High Point Stories. 69
25) January 30, 1984–Airplane Crash 79
26) Growing Pains As a Widow 85
27) Events After Clyde Went To Heaven 89
28) Remembrances by Family and Friends. 97
29) Lessons From Living Life 107
30) Pastor James Denny's 1984 Memorial Day Message. 109

Endorsements

By Dr. Gerald Parker

Clyde–the Big Brother

I grew up in the shadow of my brother, eight years my senior. I'm sure I was a major pest. Clyde was called by God in the eighth grade to preach. As we grew older, I began to realize how purposeful he was–even passionate as the two of us would go to these little churches to sing together and for him to preach

As we matured, I remember being amazed just how much he could accomplish and I often said, *"Clyde would do more before breakfast than I could get done all day."* He not only had dreams for himself, but for me and others. I often wondered, from where did this energy come? He would see a need or opportunity, then design a plan, excite others to participate and later in life, find and delegate awesome leadership to make it happen. But we all knew, his vision made the difference.

Can you imagine the feelings of inadequacy when I compared myself to my big brother? He encouraged me to think BIG, even asked me for advise with establishing small Bible Study groups, since that was a part of my experience.

As the LORD helped me grow up, in my 30s and 40s, I realized He gifted me differently and comparisons were sin. I learned to celebrate with great pride the gifts He gave my brother.

I remember after his home going–some men with whom I knew Clyde had disagreements, these men shared with me that Clyde would follow-up with them expressing that he knew they did not agree on some decisions, but that he loved them.... Clyde Alfred Parker was real, no pretense, he genuinely cared for others–loved being part of building the Kingdom and leaving a legacy that gives praise to our LORD.

Dr. Gerald Parker,
retired Professor Appalachian State University

By Dr. Brian Donley

The daily drive past the church office at 5:00 a.m. always saw the lights on in Dr. Clyde Parker's office. He was preparing his Sunday sermon, his lectures for the classes he taught at Winston Salem State University, and checking the hospital admissions records for any of his flock that might have been hospitalized overnight or awaiting surgery.

Before rushing off to class he made his hospital rounds and when classes were over, he was making pastoral calls and home visits to his church members. As senior pastor of one of the largest churches in High Point, Dr. Parker was one of the most energetic, compassionate, and committed Christian leaders I had ever met.

Endorsements

He chaired the Board of Trustees of John Wesley College and was the driving force behind its successful relocation of the College from Greensboro to its new campus in High Point.

Dr. Parker was a remarkable man as a Pastor, a Professor in Higher Education, a Christian businessman, and visionary. His visionary abilities and passion encouraged, inspired and grew First Wesleyan Church, and started the Wesleyan Arms Retirement, the Wesleyan Education Center, and every other organization he touched.

He was deeply admired and respected in the community and was a man whose commitment to Christ was unquestionable. Our hearts wept at his passing, but his Christian leadership will never be forgotten .

Dr. Brian Donley,
former President John Wesley College,
Trustee Board Member of River Landing
Retirement Community

By Ed Winslow

Dr. Clyde Parker led me in the sinner's prayer when I was a young man. Now, at 72 years of age I am considered an old man. As I look back over many years of doing my best to serve God I ask myself this question. Besides my wife and the Lord, who has had the greatest influence on my life? By far, this man was Dr. Clyde Parker. I consider him my spiritual father.

I watched him as he labored day and night to minister to the needs of people. He went door to door with us as we ministered to our bus ministry children.

He led the church in the development of our retirement center and nursing home complex. On the other side of our church campus he had the vision to start a day care and Christian school that educates children from birth through high school graduation, all in a Christian environment. Today, it ministers to over a thousand children and youth every year, and is one of the largest Christian Schools in North Carolina.

He was one of the leaders in the North Carolina East District of the Wesleyan Church in the development of a camp for children and youth. This was at a time when the emphasis was on building adult camps not camps for children. Today Victory Mountain Camp ministers to hundreds of children and teens every year. The list of Clyde's accomplishments is a long one!

Clyde's vision, his wisdom, his kindness, his love for others and his love for Christ had a profound influence on my life. As a young Christian I wanted to be just like Clyde.

As you read the story of his life in this book I hope that it will encourage you in your walk with Christ. Clyde Parker knew that **"all things are possible with Christ."**

Ed Winslow,
Retired Professor,
Randolph County Community College

Endorsements

By Joel Farlow

In serving as the Head of School at Wesleyan Christian Academy for thirty-three years, I had the opportunity to work with many wonderful individuals, but working with Dr. Clyde Parker, who was the founder of the Academy, was an outstanding experience. His love for Christ and Christ's church were clearly the core of his life.

He possessed amazing visionary skills combined with good practical business expertise. Added to these wonderful talents was a very high energy level. His accomplishments were amazing.

It was a privilege and honor to have worked with Clyde and to have had such a very special friend. The pages of this book will reaffirm these wonderful qualities, as well as many other attributes.

Joel Farlow,
Head of School, Wesleyan Christian Academy
Ministry of First Wesleyan Church, High Point, NC

Foreword

By Ronnel Stephen Parker, Sr

For as long as I can remember, my Mother and Dad modeled Jesus to me in the most incredible ways. I knew Jesus was their Savior and I knew He was their Friend, but the most important thing I remember about them was that Jesus was their King.

Ever so often I will hear my grandkids say to each other *"you're not the boss of me"*. My parents always made me believe that Jesus was "the boss of them". It took me thirty years to come to that point where Jesus was the King of my life.

Life could have been so much easier for my parents but they chose to live a life that was a complete abandonment of themselves so that they could give themselves away to those around them.

I will always love and cherish the memories and consistent life they lived completely yielded to King Jesus.

Preface

MEMORY IS A part of our human experience that makes our life rich with warm fuzzies... laughter and tears of joy as we recall the past and honor the memory of those who have gone on to heaven.

If we fail to recall the past, if we fail to pass on our rich heritage to each succeeding generation, we will destroy what our ancestors worked so hard to gain. That which kept our forefathers strong when life was hard.
Judges 2:10 says, *"... another generation grew up, who knew neither the Lord, nor what He had done for Israel."* How was such a thing possible? It is possible when the stories are not passed down from generation to generation. Are we on purpose passing on to the next generation the stories of miraculous happenings in our lives and in the lives of our parents and grandparents? Are our children and grandchildren going to know, and pass on to their children these stories so they can draw strength from their christian heritage?

We have the material means to smother our children and grandchildren with gifts. We lovingly leave them precious heirlooms, tucked away in the dusty trunks and boxes in the attic. However, Judges 2 is reminding us that the **spiritual legacy** we leave them is the **most important!**

Timothy's grandmother, Lois and his mother Eunice must have shared spiritual treasures with him according to II Timothy 1:5. Paul said of Timothy, *"I know that you sincerely trust in the Lord for you have the faith of your mother, Eunice, and your grandmother, Lois."*

CLYDE A. PARKER Sr. EdD; DD
40 years in Christian Ministry
30 years an Educator
25 years a Businessman

Introduction

YOU HAVE HEARD of the proverbial cat with nine lives? Clyde Parker lived **three** concurrent lives. His first calling to be a pastor and father started in his late teens. His second and third concurrent lives started in his early and late twenties!! Clyde's multi-faceted, productive life was described at his Memorial Service in February, 1984 by the following speakers: Dr. Virgil Mitchell, Dr. Viola Britt, Rev. James Denny, and Dr. Douglas Covington and Dr. Melvin Gadson, both from WSSU. This compilation of what they said is on Clyde's grave cover in High Point Memorial Park. May these words whet your appetite to read the rest of this book.

"Dr. Clyde Parker was a preacher, a pastor, a churchman, a teacher, a trustee, an educator, an administrator, a public servant, a humanitarian, a leader, a businessman, a manager, a dreamer, a motivator, an innovator, a communicator, a counselor, a loyal friend, a devoted husband, a loving father, and a Christian gentleman extraordinary.

Pursuit of excellence was the goal of Clyde Parker. It was a way of life with him. He could engage in many enterprises concurrently and yet do each of them exceptionally well. He had special gifts to analyze situations and arrive at good solutions. He was a crusader for what he felt to be right. He possessed a clear understanding of the Scriptural teaching on ministering to the total person... heart, mind, and body. To him, evangelism and social action were clearly combined.

Endowed with a great mind and a loving spirit, he was constantly giving, yet demanded so little from others. There was a side of him which resisted recognition. Only those who know him best had any idea how much he gave without wanting credit for it. He was optimistic about God's work, yet had a constructive discontent with the status quo. He was known and respected for his sound judgment and belief that the Lord's work should be done first class!

As a master-teacher, he was a shining example of professionalism and educational excellence in the field of teacher education. He was always one to offer praise, encouragement and reassurance. He inspired others to rise above adversity. He cared about his fellow man and was strong enough and secure enough to show it.

In his many-faceted, admirable career, he maintained a strong sense of humility. His success was the result of his ability to work "with" people, rather than to insist on the trappings of leadership. He accomplished so much in such a short time. He lived under the compulsion that he had a Divine Master to serve; a Divine Mission to accomplish; a Divine Message to proclaim. He has been released from his labors, but his works follow him. 'The light of the righteous shines brightly.'"

Chapter 1
We Were Born In North Carolina "Mill" Towns

In late 1930 I was born in the small cotton mill town of Randleman, North Carolina where my Dad pastored a small church. The parsonage beside the church, was a former "mill house" but was adequate for the Phillips family of two little daughters.

Clyde Parker was born a few months later in Kannapolis, another very unusual mill town owned by the Cannon family. Hundreds of small homes for the mill "hands" were built by Mr. Cannon. Water and electricity were furnished and rent was very low for the small houses. Kannapolis was named for the Cannon family who owned all the down town businesses as well as the small houses. The town remained unincorporated for many decades! Churches of various denominations were scattered along the streets of Kannapolis.

Clyde's mother, Gladys, worked in the mill sitting at a sewing machine all day hemming towels. Clyde's Dad, Roy Lee, also worked for the mill as a painter. Teams of men kept the houses and businesses painted neatly by working all year. Kannapolis was a neat clean little town that seemed to have no slums.

Clyde's grandfather, Willie Parker and his wife lived on a farm near Richfield, plowing the garden with horses to raise vegetables from the stubborn red soil. The two cows supplied milk for the growing Parker family. Chickens laid eggs, then became meat along with rabbits and other forest animals for their family of five children: Henry D.; Annie Lou; Carrie Mae; Dole Unie and Roy Lee. Electricity had not come down their country road, so after dark, the lamps were lit for all evening indoor family activities. Lanterns lit the path to do the barn chores during the dark early Winter evenings.

A few miles down the dirt road the Glover family was raising their family of two girls, Gladys and Bethel, on their farm near the St. Paul Pilgrim Holiness Church. The Glover family was known throughout the whole community as kind, committed, loyal members of that church. Grandmother Emma Glover graciously made the Glover home the hospitality center where any visiting clergy stayed overnight.

In the early 1900s my Grandpa Will and Viola Phillips farm was down the dirt road near High Falls. Grandpa built the four room unpainted farm house but added two more small bedrooms as their family grew. My Dad, Roy, was the second son in their family of five daughters and five sons. As the years went by, four of their sons became pastors and one daughter became a pastor's wife, a sterling reflection of their parent's consistent committed Christian lives.

The following story confirms the deeply committed Christian lives the Phillips parents passed on to their family of ten children. Their two young sons, Roy and Paul were helping their Dad clear some new ground, when his axe slipped and split his leg open clear to the bone. While he sat holding the wound together he sent Roy to the house for a needle and white thread and some brown paper. Paul went to find some rosin from the nearby pine trees.

Sitting on a tree stump with his two young sons watching in wide-eyed wonder, their Dad sewed his leg wound shut, treating it with prayer and pine rosin, then covering it with the brown paper. Leaning on his two sons as if they were crutches, he managed to get home from the forest and the wound healed in time.

Chapter 2
Living Conditions On A Farm In The 1900s

Growing up in a North Carolina farm home in Gold Hill and Richfield, for Roy and Gladys Parker must have been very much like G'pa Will and G'ma Viola Phillip's farm home in High Falls. My sister, Leuola and I spent some nights at G'pa Will and G'ma Viola'a farm home in the mid 1930s. Leuola imagined what it might have been when our parents were little children:

> *"The bedroom last night was freezing cold, but the homemade quilts kept you warm. The mattress was like a bed-sized pillowcase stuffed with straw, lumpy and scratchy. You must be careful, running to the fireplace, because you might get a splinter in your feet, because the floors are wooden planks. The fireplace rug is rags that have been braided together.*
>
> *Grab the clothes you wore to school yesterday and dress in front of the fireplace. The same clothes are worn all week, unless they get really dirty. You only have two or three school clothes and one good dress to wear to church. Mom makes all the clothes you wear and knits your socks and stockings.*

Once a week she washes clothes on a washboard in water she pulled out of the well. Someone would build a fire under a BIG black wash pot in the yard so she could scrub the clothes clean with a bar of soap. She rinsed the clothes, then draped them over the bushes to dry. Some time later G'pa made her a clothes line. When it rained, she would dry them by the fireplace."

We actually experienced a lot of those activities in the 1930s when we visited G'pa and G'ma Will Phillip's farm home at High Falls!! Our Daddy told us G'pa always got up early to build the kitchen stove fire, while G'ma made biscuits and gravy for breakfast to go with the homemade jam, milk, butter and boiled eggs. Since there was no electricity, the lamp on the table cast long shadows against the wall because it was still dark outside. In the winter the children walked to school in the dark so the oldest child carried the lantern so they could see, AND to scare any wild animals away. Some families had an extra horse for their children to ride to school.

Daddy Roy Phillips told us children how a young man stopped him and his horse one day, going home from school, and tried to force him to drink some "moonshine". Remembering his promise, that he would never start "drinking", he spurred his horse, and away he sped for home. He told his mother what had just happened and, as she had promised, she reached high on the top shelf into a small container, and handed him a shiny new silver dollar. He was a happy young teenage boy. My grandmother, Viola, was a very wise mother to her ten children!

The one room school was already warm when the children arrived because the teacher came early to start a fire in the stove. She taught all classes from 1st through 8th grades in the same room. The students did their own assignments with the teacher going from one group to another. Sometimes younger children listened to the older students lessons and learned hard stuff.

Back home, each child had chores to do before starting homework. The wood and kindling must be brought in to keep the fires going. The children helped Dad milk the cows, feed the livestock and "slop" the hogs. They also pulled up buckets of water out of the well.

The big tea kettle whistled on the stove with hot water to wash dishes and take "spit" baths after supper. Homework was done by lamp light or the fireplace light. Dad would read from the Bible and everybody prayed. Warm flannel gowns were put on before going to bed in that COLD bedroom. Mom gave each one a bottle filled with hot water to warm their feet under the mountain of quilts. Sweet dreams!!!

My Dad told us about the Christmas trees they had when he was a boy. Since there was no electricity, the little cedar tree, cut from the forest around them, was decorated with homemade candles. On Christmas Eve, the candles were placed in the tree in little holders that clamped onto a branch. The holders were much like a little girl's hair barrette. Roy and Gladys Parker no doubt made the same kind of tree decorations when they were little children living in their farm home.

On Christmas Eve the candles were lit with matches. G'pa and the boys would watch carefully and put out any fires in the tree branches. The family would sing Christmas carols and enjoy the tree until the candles burned dangerously low. That is hard for us to even imagine!!

Chapter 3
Early years of Roy and Hannah Phillips

Intercept with Footsteps of Parker and Glover Families

Roy Phillips' Quaker pastor in High Falls, NC had graduated from The Training School for Christian Workers, in Huntington Park, California. He recommended that Roy travel by train to California and attend the same school. Roy's mother, Viola, packed a lard bucket full of biscuits, baked sweet and white potatoes and etc, so he would have food for the week long train ride. When he arrived at the school, he took his lard bucket to the dining room to share,... but no one wanted any of his "left-overs"!

While a student at TSCW, Roy met Hannah Dorothy Schendel, whose parents had migrated from Germany and settled in California. After graduation, Hannah came East and worked in a Boarding School for African American students in western North Carolina. Several months later, Roy also came to the same school to teach. Unfortunately, two of the young boys were such mischief makers, the Principal expelled them. Roy Phillips took them in his T Model Ford to the train station, and bought tickets for them to go to Winston Salem where they lived. Roy did not stay long enough to make sure they actually got on the train, so the two boys walked back to the school in the dark, and after midnight they set on fire the wood that was stacked under the dormitory.

The dormitory was an old wooden structure that burned easily and quickly. By a miracle, all of the girls and women teachers got out safely. However, Hannah was throwing things out of her window before she escaped down the stairs that were beginning to burn. The building collapsed just as she got to the bottom of the stairs!!

Roy and Hannah were engaged to be married weeks later, but... since her home was in California, he drove the two of them to High Falls, in his T Model Ford. The next day they were married in the parlor of the Phillips farm home. Roy's sister, Daisy helped with decorating the parlor using pink and white crepe paper. Daisy also played on the pump organ, *"Bless Be The Tie That Binds"* and the Justice of the Peace married them, because Roy's pastor was away from home, on a trip.

The North Carolina Pilgrim Holiness District Superintendent, Rev. S.M. Stikeleather, lived in Kentucky and traveled to North Carolina, and from church to church in his BIG Packard automobile. He asked Roy and Hannah Phillips if they would pastor the Gold Hill/St. Paul Pilgrim Holiness Churches. The little village of Gold Hill had become famous for the discovery of gold, in the late 1800s. The "get rich quick miners" had dug many under ground tunnels with axes and shovels. That's hard for us to even imagine, but remember that was before mechanized digging machines.

It was at this point in time when Roy and Hannah Phillips' lives crossed the paths of Roy Parker and Gladys Glover. Roy Parker's family attended the Gold Hill Pilgrim Church and Glady Glover's family were members of the St. Paul Pilgrim Church. The churches were only a few miles apart on the dirt roads.

Chapter 4
Christian Schools in the 1920s

Phillips, Parker and Glover Families Meet

In the late 1920s, Roy and Hannah Phillips, became pastors of the St. Paul/Gold Hill circuit of churches. A former pastor had started a school in a building beside the Gold Hill church, that included an elementary, middle school and high school. Roy Phillips became Principal of the student body of fifty-one students. He also taught Bible, Mathematics and Doctrine. Vera M. Davie taught High School; Dovie Wagoner taught Intermediate classes; and Hannah Phillips taught the elementary grades and **Gladys Glover was one of her students.**

The low cost of attending a christian school 100 years ago is hard to even imagine. I discovered, on the back of a student body picture, that day students paid $1.50 or $2.00 a month, which is what the Glover parents paid for their two girls to get a christian education. They sometimes let Bethel drive herself and Gladys in their T model Ford the few miles to school.

Gladys Glover and Roy Lee Parker met when they were teenagers through some Youth or Revival meetings shared by both churches. After a few months of dating, quiet Roy got up the nerve and asked Gladys to marry him while they were still teenagers. They were married after one of the Sunday morning worship services.

What a wonderful way to marry with all your friends together, and not having to decorate the church for a wedding!

Roy and Gladys Parker moved to Kannapolis, a mill town to get jobs in the Cannon Mill Manufacturing company. Walking in her mother Emma Glover's footsteps, Gladys made their home, with Roy's help, the hospitality center for visiting preachers who came to preach at their Kannapolis church. They were known for their delicious meals and overnight accommodations.

Chapter 5
The Roy Phillips Family Keeps Moving

Hannah Phillips had to quit teaching at the Gold Hill Christian School when their first child, Leuola, was born in May, 1928. A year later the District Superintendent, Rev. S.M. Stikeleather wanted Roy and Hannah to pastor the Pilgrim Holiness Church in the small "cotton mill" town of Randleman

In December 1930 their second daughter, Ernstena, was born. As time moved on, the tabernacle beside the Randleman church became an excellent place for Leuola and Ernstena to play "church". Leuola would be the preacher and Ernstena would go to the altar to pray for salvation!

Daddy Roy Phillips took the family to California, every four years as he had promised Hannah, to visit her Schendel family members. When I was in the third or fourth grade, our quadrennium trip made a little detour into Mexico, all the way to Mexico City. We stayed with missionaries along the way. On Sunday morning, the missionaries and our family rode horses to a thatched roof, dirt floor church tucked away in the forest. There were no roads through the forests to villages, but the horse trails led to tiny villages. My horse had a baby pony tied beside it, so the mama horse would not run away with me!! That was a "scary" bumpy horse ride for me!!

On each of the quadrennium trips, Daddy wanted to expose his children to more adventures than just traveling across the United States. One trip we took the northern route through the northern states. Another time we went straight across the United States stopping to see important history sites along the way. We were never allowed to take naps in the car, because we would miss something! Our Daddy was a great teacher!

Not many families in the late 1930s, early 1940s traveled by car across the country like our family did. The Fall after our quadrennial trip, my teacher found out we had traveled into Mexico going to California, so she asked me to tell the class about my adventures. She made a lesson in Geography by pointing on a big map, with her "pointer", the places I had visited and was describing to them.

Chapter 6
Parker Family Living in Kannapolis–Cannon Family's Mill Town

"Mill Villages" in the 1930s and 1940s were unique neighborhoods. When Roy and Gladys got married and moved to Kannapolis, they lived in one of the tiny four room "mill houses" a few years.

In the early 1930s one of their Gold Hill church friends challenged Roy and Gladys to let him build a "stone" house, at a modest cost, which would become a model home of his work in Kannapolis and surrounding area. Interestingly, the six room house had no closets as we have today. The closet door opened to a tiny opening with large nails driven into the back wall from which you could hang your clothes!! It had electricity and running water, so there was a small toilet room for the commode, sink, and tiny bathtub. It did indeed become a model home for the people in that part of Kannapolis.

Community life in the "mill villages" revolved for the most part around the church and church activities. People didn't even lock their doors because neighbors respected and looked after each other. Children walked to and from school. If children misbehaved when they were away from home, other parents would scold them and the child's parents appreciated it. Children were expected to live by the "golden rule." ***Do unto others as you would have them do unto you.***

A couple years after Clyde entered school he had a bad case of dyptheria causing him to miss several weeks of school. He struggled to keep up with his class academically which almost kept him from being promoted to the next class in Elementary School. Even so, he never lost sight of the fact that some day he wanted to go to college.

Their pastor's daughter, Mildred Page, wrote Clyde a letter when she was attending a Christian High School in Kentucky. The envelope was dated February 6, 1942 and sent with a 3 cent stamp!! On the back of that small empty envelope, Clyde had written in legible cursive: *"Mother, me and Gerald have gone to take my music. I clean him up good, Clyde P.S. We have ate and I clean the dishes. So you go on and eat."* Clyde would have been eleven, almost twelve years old! He was an incredibly thoughtful son and big brother to his younger brother.

Try to imagine Clyde and Gerald riding on a bicycle, several miles on a two-lane road between his house and his piano teacher's home in Landis. Clyde didn't want to leave his four year old brother at home alone. If I remember correctly, Roy and Gladys had a lady who came to their home after school to be with the boys until they got home from work, so that must have been a day she couldn't come. Clyde wanted so badly to learn to play the piano which he thought would help him in Ministry as he grew older.

In early Spring when Clyde was eleven or twelve years of age, his Dad would help him plant tomato seeds. As the plants grew, Clyde would carefully take them out with a little bit of dirt clinging to the roots, and sell the plants to neighbors. He would take the family push mower and mow neighbor's yards, or offer to do odd jobs for neighbors and church friends. He was determined to make a little bit of money to help his parents. Roy and Gladys knew their preteen son was different from most boys they knew in the "mill village".

Chapter 7
Clyde's Musical Abilities Grow

An evangelist and wife came for a Revival at Clyde's church, and the husband played an accordion when they sang together. That sparked a desire in Clyde's heart to play an accordion to help him in his future ministry. His parents found a man in Concord who agreed to give him lessons, so they bought a cheap accordion and drove him each week for lessons. He learned so quickly, his parents decided to buy him an expensive Excelsior accordion that cost as much as some cars! Clyde protested that he didn't need such an expensive accordion, but they told him they wanted to give it to him as his high school graduation gift! They were so very proud of their most unusual son. After thinking it over, Clyde concluded he would earn enough money to buy a car, but he would not spend that much money on an accordion.

He was going to school full-time and selling vacuum cleaners, and **did** buy a little Starlite Coupe Studebaker. Incidentally the accordion, in the 2020s, is still making beautiful music in the hands of granddaughters, Sydney and Shelby, Clyde Jr. and Kim Parker's daughters.

There was a group called "The Cracker Jacks" on Charlotte's WBTV in the 1940s. Television was only in black and white and came on in late afternoon and evening hours. It was the only station on Gladys and Roy Parker's television set. Someone told Arthur

Smith, of The Cracker Jacks, about Clyde's ability to play the Excelcior accordion, and after interviewing him, he asked Clyde to come play "The Heaven Train" on their TV show. Surprising everyone, Arthur Smith asked if he would start playing with their band on the "Cracker Jacks" TV show. Clyde explained to me years later, he was tempted, but he did NOT want to become distracted from his call to be a preacher. It was pretty amazing that a teenager was able to walk away from something so exciting as being on a very popular television program. His call to be a preacher, when he was twelve years old, remained his goal in life even with many distractions.

Chapter 8
Driver's License at Fifteen

Clyde Parker started preaching before he was old enough to get driver's license. Dad, Roy, would drive him all around the state, wherever he had been invited to preach. After his 15th birthday, Clyde got his license. The age had been lowered for the convenience of families whose teen age sons were enlisting in the armed forces. Shortly after getting his license, Roy and Gladys allowed him to drive their only car. At times his friend, Reese Allred, would accompany that red-haired "boy preacher" from the Kannapolis church, on these sometimes weekly trips to preach.

Clyde told me his first sermon was: *"Does the devil have a forked tail, eyes of fire and chains around his feet?"* After we were married I remember laughing and asking him to explain what on earth that meant! He referred me to Genesis 3 and explained that if the devil was scary looking Eve would never have listened to him. Satan is smart and is still deceiving people. He comes to us as an angel of light with half truths, planting desires in our mind. It was an eye opening message coming from that "boy preacher"!!

Interestingly, Clyde's pastor, Rev. W.F. Page was so proud of the "boy preacher" in his church, that he and the local church board voted to issue Local Preacher License to Clyde at fourteen. He had the distinction of the being the youngest Licensed Preacher in the District,... ever.

The young "mill hill" teenage bullies decided it was their job to tease and pick fights with that red-haired "preacher boy". Clyde would walk home from school different ways, trying to avoid being beat up and having his clothes torn or his hair pulled. Clyde learned early how Christians can be persecuted for their faith.

He seemed aware many times that the Lord was providing protection for him from other students or adults along the street. I think there were probably many times that Clyde felt the supernatural power of the Hand of God on him.

Chapter 9
College Plans Almost Torpedoed

CLYDE'S EIGHTH-GRADE TEACHER was calling students, individually, to her desk to discuss their academic abilities. She would explain why she was assigning them to take, in the 9th grade, the "regular" courses, business classes, or college-prep courses. Clyde explained he wanted to be a preacher so he needed to have college-prep classes in high school. *"No, Clyde my decision is final! As I told you before, I cannot let you sign up for college-prep course for high school next year because your grades are not good enough."*

The withering gaze and searing words of the teacher produced a snickering ripple across the classroom of listening classmates, who were supposed to be reading an assignment. The thirteen year old's cheeks and ears flushed to the color of his red hair, and his shoulders sagged a bit, but disappointment and refusal fueled the fire of determination in the heart of the slender freckle-faced Clyde.

He had accepted the Lord as his personal Savior at age 12 and very soon after felt a "call" to be a preacher. It was this single-mindedness that made him determined to go to college, quite an ambition for a poor boy whose parents only finished the third and eighth grades. In fact, there was no one in his family's history who had finished high school, much less gone to college.

As he trudged home from school that day, his mind forged a plan, a plan so radical, he wondered if his parents could be convinced. Not to worry! His persuasive power convinced them to let him attend a Christian boarding high school in Frankfort, Indiana to get the college prep courses he needed despite his poor grades.

Most churches in the early to mid 1900s had what they called the "Amen" corner at the front of the church sanctuary where older men sat and encouraged their pastor shouting out, *"Amen"*. It was interesting that after God called Clyde to preach, he started sitting in the Amen Corner which led the way for younger men to also join the older men.

Another phenomenon of that period of time, was "street preaching". Sometimes during his mid-teen years, Clyde was asked to preach on the street corner in some of the cities where he was asked to preach in a church. It was a curiosity in most cities to see a teenager preaching with such fervor.

Chapter 10
Clyde's Busy Mid-Teens

IN SEPTEMBER, FIVE months after his fourteenth birthday, Clyde's persuasive power convinced his parents to let him attend the Christian boarding High School in Indiana to get the college-prep courses he needed despite his poor grades. His sacrificing parents saw him off at the bus station, with his packed suitcase, and he traveled by bus to Frankfort, Indiana to a Bible School that also had a high school division.

Two young married men from his Kannapolis church were enrolled in the Bible School which made it a little easier for Roy and Gladys to make the decision for Clyde to go. Their foresight and faith were quite amazing considering their meager wages from the cotton-mill, and their limited experience in traveling. Their only other child, Gerald, was seven years old.

Coming home from Indiana, the next Summer, he got his driver's license at age fifteen.

Clyde investigated where the Kannapolis City Schools had classes for students with poor or failing grades so they could make up school work, and took as many classes as they would allow. In September, 1946, Kernersville Pilgrim Bible School opened, also having Jr. College and high school classes, so he transferred there. Graduating from high school in 1948, a month after his 17th birthday, he started attending Catawba College taking as many Summer classes as they would allow.

In addition to going to Summer School, he started selling Elecrolux Vacuum Cleaners. He would borrow the one family car and sell vacuum cleaners in the neighboring towns and villages and Roy and Gladys would walk home from their mill jobs. That was a startling illustration of what sacrificing parents they were, helping their God-called preacher boy.

The funniest story from his selling days, happened in a home where they were raising baby chickens. He was demonstrating how the power of the machine to blow away was as powerful as it's suction. In his zeal he forgot to plug the hose to the blowing side and unfortunately sucked a tiny baby chicken into the machine's trash bag. Quickly changing the hose to the blowing side he blew that baby chick out across the room, then vacuuming the dirt that had come out with the baby chicken. They bought the machine, and they had no carpets, only wood floors! In later life, we laughed lots of times about that poor, little, baby chicken!!

As a teenager and working only part-time, he was such a good salesman, he won several prizes for the home, like an expensive electric food mixer. His mother, however, refused to use any prizes he won, saying he needed to save them for when he got married. To remember the sacrificing mother Gladys Parker was brings tears to my eyes!

Chapter 11
Married at Eighteen

CLYDE COMPLETED HIS Jr. College work at the Kernersville Bible School by the time I was graduating from High School. Three months after Clyde's 18th birthday, we were married August 4, 1949, in the Roanoke Pilgrim Holiness church where my Dad, Roy Phillips, was pastor.

During that Summer I made my white, satin, long wedding dress as well as the long veil with a valentine-shaped head piece! It was my own little miracle that I had won a little Singer Spinnet sewing machine in the Spring of 1949. I had visited the store one day, so my name was in the pot, **only one time**, to win the sewing machine!! It was extra special making my wedding dress on my very own electric sewing machine!!

Gladys was a VERY unselfish mother, always pushing her two boys and providing them affirmations. Be sure to read the Endorsement Clyde's brother, Gerald, wrote in the front of this book. Gerald is now a retired professor from Appalachian State Teacher's University in Boone, NC.

Clyde continued selling Elecrolux Vacuum Cleaners into the first year we were married, while he was also attending Marion College, now Indiana Wesleyan University, in Marion, Indiana.

We found a little two-room apartment for $1.00 a day. Bill and Alma Terry from Louisville, KY, lived in the other two upstairs rooms and we all shared the same bathroom on the first floor. Alma worked in a Finance Company in downtown Marion and recommended me to be secretary to one of the loan officers where I made $37 a week. Bill and Alma remained wonderful life-long friends.

Mother Gladys and Dad Roy Parker would surprise us occasionally with a check for us to have some extra money! Clyde worked odd jobs to make a few dollars and still attended all his classes. He was indeed an incredible teenager and now head of his household!

In 1949 for our first Christmas together in Marion, Indiana, Clyde wanted a tree, but we didn't have the money to buy one. He went to the forest and found a little "Charlie Brown" cedar tree. Clyde couldn't figure out how to make it stand up straight, so he just nailed it to the wood floor...no damage done, really.

We didn't have money to buy electric lights and colored balls, so I strung popcorn with a needle and thread into a chain. I also made a paper chain with colored paper. We laughed and laughed about our first Christmas tree. It really did brighten our spirits in that tiny two-room apartment.

When we returned from our North Carolina Christmas vacation, our little tree was dried up and bent almost to the floor and some strange little insects had taken over our kitchen. Apparently some tiny insect eggs had hatched in our warm apartment while we were gone. Clyde got rid of those bugs in a hurry with some spray.

Chapter 12
Clyde's First Pastorate at Nineteen

On Clyde's nineteenth birthday, he started pastoring a church in the rich farm-land, of Swayzee, Indiana, a few miles outside Marion. The church gave him a few dollars each week for being their pastor. The farmers also give us farm vegetables and fruits which helped with our grocery needs. The congregation grew the year Clyde was their pastor. They really seemed to love and appreciate their teenage pastor.

One Sunday we were invited to eat Sunday lunch with one of the farm families. We were enjoying the afternoon when suddenly, Clyde remembered he had invited a couple to eat supper with us and **he had forgotten to tell me!!** We quickly excused ourselves and left in our little Studebaker car.

I was horrified and angry with him. We didn't have anything prepared, and our little two-room apartment was very messy! What was I going to do? I cried!! When we arrived at the apartment, our guests, had arrived and our friends, Bill Terry and Fred Hill were sitting on the porch visiting with them. We greeted them and Clyde sat down while I dashed upstairs to my kitchen.

There were Alma and Doris busy at work. They had cleaned the apartment and prepared supper! When our guests had arrived, Bill and Alma guessed Clyde had forgotten to tell me, so Bill went to get Doris and Fred to help. (We had no telephones, so Bill had to go get them.) I had nothing to cook, so Alma and Doris had made sandwiches and jello for dessert. The Terrys and Hills were our very BEST FRIENDS.

Ronnie was born June 1951, a month after Clyde graduated from Marion college...an unusual graduation present. My doctor did NOT want us traveling back to North Carolina until Ronnie was six weeks old, so we moved in July. By then we were both twenty years old.

Chapter 13
Back Home In North Carolina

WE MOVED BACK to N. C. with Ronnie our five weeks old baby. The doctor in Marion who had delivered Ronnie kept me in the hospital a week and did not want me traveling for a month after his birth!

The District Superintendent had sent word that the little country Pilgrim Church on a dirt cross road at Harmony village, near Mocksville, NC asked us to be their pastor. The old wooden church building appeared as if it were ready to fall down if a strong wind were to blow. The foundation corners of the church were sitting on large rocks.

There were no Sunday school classrooms, no air conditioning and heat for the winter months came from a wood burning stove in the middle of the church. With Clyde's encouragement, that congregation decided they needed to build a new church. Within weeks, the church board, made up of elderly old people, voted to build a new church. There were perhaps a dozen young adults and as many children in the congregation.

I still marvel that a twenty year old young man was able to get that small congregation of older people to follow his recommendations.

Clyde started visiting every farmer in the community, asking for trees to build a new church. Many volunteered! Clyde and the farmers, carrying saws and leading the horses, went into the woods to cut down trees that were given to build the new church. They hitched the cut trees behind horses which pulled them to the side of the road. The logs were then hauled to the church yard and put into a BIG pile.

A saw mill was brought to the church yard and the workers began cutting up the trees into lumber. The bark side was sliced off first until the log was square. Then back through the saw mill, the tree was cut into boards. The person that carried away the slices of bark and pieces of lumber was called the "off bearer". That was the hardest job of all.

The saw mill men and farmers decided to play a trick on that young, energetic, red-headed, "city slicker" preacher, so they asked him to be the off-bearer. They worked fast and furious cutting the slabs and boards. It was a hot day and Clyde was running back and forth pulling and carrying the boards and slabs out of the way. When they saw he was about to faint from heat and exhaustion, they told him, *"We just wanted to see if you can work as hard as we can."* Laughing they told him he had passed their test!! **"You're a good preacher and a hard worker."**

A nice seven room parsonage was beside the church, but there was no sink with running water in the kitchen and there was no bathroom. In the back yard was the little one seater "outhouse" at the edge of the woods.

A well on the back porch was where we got all the water we needed. It took lots of buckets of water to fill the "wringer" washing machine to wash Ronnie's cloth diapers. There were NO disposable diapers in those days, only cloth diapers.

One day we got a letter in our road-side mail box addressed: Clyde Parker, High Point, North Carolina. It was from an elderly member of the Swayzee, Indiana church, where we had pastored, who **thought** we lived in High Point. We scratched our heads trying to figure out how on earth did somebody in the High Point post office know to scribble our Harmony, NC address on the envelope!

Years later when we moved to High Point we discovered how we got that letter. The Assistant Post Master in High Point, a Mr. Winslow, was a member of First Wesleyan Church, and was a delegate to Conference. He had remembered the name Clyde Parker who was introduced as a new pastor, so he found our address in the District Minutes and forwarded it to us. Some public servants are extremely kind!!

One day I was burning trash beside the path to the "outhouse". I had not noticed that the wind was blowing. Oh, dear!! The fire began to spread to the dry leaves. Clyde was not home, so I ran to the shed for a rake, but that wasn't helping. Baby Ronnie was in the house in his play pen. I wasn't worried about him, but I was worried a lot about the spreading fire. I raced to the back porch to pull up a bucket of water. With the dipper I poured dribbles of water on the leaves to wet them, but that wasn't stopping the fire from spreading.

I cried and prayed, *"Oh Jesus, help me, if You don't help me, the woods will burn, the neighbor's barn will burn and maybe the parsonage.* **Please** *help me dear Jesus."* I was astonished as the wind quit blowing and the fire quit spreading. Then I began crying and thanking Jesus for answering my prayer. God was so good to take care of my silly mistake.

Chapter 14
Parker's Motel

Clyde's parents attended his graduation from Marion College (now Indiana Wesleyan University) in 1951 and stayed in a little strip motel just outside Marion, Indiana. An idea popped into Clyde's head, and he shared the idea with his parents. If they built a strip motel in Kannapolis, N.C. it would be a wonderful way they could quit working at Cannon Mill. Clyde was a busy, just-turned-twenty-year old, but even so he was thinking of ways to help his parents leave the mill work and get into some kind of business.

Back in North Carolina, Clyde asked my father, Roy Phillips, if he could loan some of the money to buy some land in Kannapolis to get the motel started! They bought a few acres of land on the north side of where their beautiful rock home was eventually built. Every Friday and Saturday, we would travel to Kannapolis, so Clyde could encourage his parents and oversee the building of Parker's Motel. At twenty years of age, Clyde was continuing his life of multi-tasking activities! We were sooo glad when it was finally built, but Dad and Mom, Roy and Gladys, continued working at the mill until the motel was profitable.

Operating the motel was a 24 hour, never ending job, while they also continued working full time at Cannon Mills. They lived a couple years, in what was temporary living quarters, in the basement of the motel. Mother Gladys would come home soaked from sweating at her job of hemming towels, and Dad Roy would be bone tired from his job of painting mill houses. They hired a lady for a few hours a day to help clean the rooms.

One Friday night we found Dad Roy and Mother Gladys SO discouraged. The road in front of the motel was being enlarged to four lanes. It had rained and rained and no one was coming across the mud to the motel, and they didn't have enough money to make their bank payment. G'pa Roy said, *"we can't pay our tithe this month!"* Clyde said, *"Dad, when I was a little boy, you told me to always give the tithe to the church first, because it belonged to God."*

Clyde challenged his Dad by saying, *"I dare you to pay your tithe and see what God will do."* His Dad was pretty grumpy as he said, *"Well, OK, we will... but you will see, we'll lose the motel if we don't pay our bills."*

The next Friday night we went to Kannapolis and Dad Roy was grinning from ear to ear. *"What has happened?"*, we excitedly asked. He answered, *"I couldn't believe it, but people started coming through the mud to get to the motel and we have enough money to pay the bank loan. I'm glad we paid our tithe first."* We, of course rejoiced with them. Before long, just as Clyde had envisioned, both of them were able to quit working at the mill which made Clyde very happy... mission accomplished.

Mother Gladys ran the intellectual side of the Motel business. She signed all the checks writing Roy's name, because he was ashamed of his scribbling signature. What a wise, loving wife she was, protecting her husband's self image. He handled the difficult side of operating the motel, running people off who had no business using motel rooms. He sometimes pulled out his little Browning .22!

Our son, Ronnie Sr., lived with them for a full Summer when he was fourteen. *"They are the kind of grandparent I want to be some day to my grandchildren."* he would comment. Ronnie Sr. and Beverly **really are** model grandparents to their grandchildren in the 2020s!

Gerald shared this funny story about his Dad's habit of hunkering down for a midnight snack. One night he slipped out of bed, made an open face peanut butter sandwich and sat down, in the dark, in his lazy boy lounge chair. Problem was... Mother Gladys had moved the furniture around. So, instead of his lazy boy, it was a rocking chair that he sat in and leaned back so fast and hard, the rocking chair went all the way over backwards!! His open face peanut sandwich landed smack on his face, eyes, hair and all!! Gladys heard the commotion and came running. It took a while before he could join her in laughing and laughing.

The next time Gerald, Mary, and their children Kim and Stan came, Grandpa immediately said, *"don't you tell them what happened to me the other night.".* Of course that opened the door for them to curiously beg Grandmother Gladys to tell them what happened. As you can imagine, there was lots of laughter.

Chapter 15
Clyde's Adventurous Children

As our children grew physically and mentally, Clyde's adventurous, leadership gene became evident in each of them. In 1954 the Elkin parsonage had a nice yard between the church and parsonage, but the narrow yard behind the parsonage plunged downhill with a little creek that became a challenge to the children.

How thrilled and relieved we were to find little Ronnie after he and his dog had gone for a walk and we thought they were lost. I even called Clyde home from teaching school to help find him. Ronnie and his dog had wandered off behind the church, down the hill, across the creek and were going up the other side. What a scary "lost child" experience that was, and all the trauma that goes with it. He knew where he was,... so why were we so frightened?!!

When Kenneth was eleven we found a note, tacked to the front door, in his sixth grade writing, telling us not to follow him, because he was leaving for the night to camp by the creek. We respected his plea for independence but, cupping my hand around my mouth so he would hear, I asked him to please come babysit with Clyde Jr, so I could play for the quartet to practice. The ghostly tree shadows were melting into the dark of night, so he came straight home, and stayed with Clyde Jr, He then decided maybe he would stay and sleep in his bed for the night..

We enrolled Phyllis in Mrs. Davis' Kindergarten class which was in the basement of her home about four houses down the street past the parsonage. She did not have much outdoor space for the children to play, front or back, so at least once each week she would take the class to the YMCA for fun exercise.

Phyllis' obsession to climb was so daring that when she got to Kindergarten, she was already experienced at climbing trees, and the tops of ball diamond backdrops, out of her Daddy's reach. The first time her class went to the YMCA for exercise was "hair-raising" scary for Mrs. Davis. Phyllis found the rope for climbing and was out of everyone's reach in no time, laughing at their efforts to talk her to come down. That was the last time Phyllis saw the gym from the rafters!! After that, before Mrs. Davis' class arrived, the rope was always pulled up out of reach.

It was a hilarious time for us all when Phyllis, as a little girl, walked on the parsonage walls. I was hoping they would never paint over those footprints, it was so much fun explaining about them. Maybe I should also explain it to you!

One afternoon Clyde and I stumbled over each other scrambling in the direction of Ronnie and Kenneth's screams. We couldn't understand their words, but it was definitely a 5 alarm distress signal. We found the boys in the narrow hall looking up with their four arms reaching as high as they could. Above them and out of reach was their little sister, her back plastered against the ceiling with her hands on one wall and her feet on the other. By the time her Daddy arrived, she was laughing so hard she was in danger of falling!!

Clyde Parker's four children are as unusual in their adult professional lives in the 2020s, as they were when they were children,... walking in their most unusual Daddy's footsteps. I like to think the Lord is letting Pepaw Clyde see his children, grandchildren and great grandchildren, committed Christians, serving as Pastors, Missionaries, Church Music Minsters, Teachers, and a University Professor.

Chapter 16
More Elkin Memories

To supplement his small salary pastoring the Elkin Pilgrim Holiness Church, Clyde got a job as a "substitute" teacher in the Elkin public schools. His empathy with the slow-learners and disadvantaged, as well as his gift of teaching, endeared him to his students and colleagues alike. Within weeks after starting as a substitute teacher, Mr. Carpenter, the Superintendent of Elkin public schools, asked him to teach a fourth grade class at North Elkin Elementary School, where the teacher had an illness that had forced her to retire early, and Clyde became the full-time teacher.

Clyde's desire for more education took him to the University of North Carolina in Greensboro, driving a hundred twenty miles, for Summer School and Saturday classes. After earning his Master's degree and Guidance Counselor's certificate, Mr. Carpenter asked him to teach in Elkin High School, and again he became a much loved teacher.

He was asked to be Elkin's first teacher to supervise teaching United States History by television. He had taken classes at UNCG from the master teacher who was chosen to be North Carolina's first teacher on television. The class originated in Greensboro and covered the North Carolina Education system. Clyde was forced to teach that TV History class in the auditorium because there were over 200 students in his television History class.

One day one of Clyde's best students came in excitedly exclaiming, *"Mr. Parker, did you know Jesus is coming back to earth some day?"* He assured her he knew because the Bible teaches that. *"But I never heard about that until last night at the crusade,"* she said. With her family she had attended the Greensboro Billy Graham Crusade. Her parents were shocked because they had never heard about Christ's 2nd coming, even though they attended church every Sunday.

The students at the high school knew Mr. Parker was a minister as well as a full time high school teacher and sometimes they asked questions about the Bible. Elkin was, and is, a small town, and fortunately, most people attended some church. However some pastors failed to teach and preach about Christ's 2nd Coming.

Clyde and I have heard about the 2nd Coming since we were little children. If people don't believe the Bible, they are cynical about Jesus' coming back to earth. Some people comment, *"Yeah... yeah... I have heard that all my life and He hasn't come back yet."*

The Bible is very clear that certain things have to happen before Jesus comes back. One of the things is that most nations of the world will turn against Israel and try to kill the Jews. The holocaust in the late 1930s and '40s, when hundreds of thousands of Jews were killed, seemed like the beginning of the end of time. The Bible is clear! He loves the Jews even though they didn't accept Him as their Messiah. He was born into a Jewish family.

<u>On a side note</u>: Norma Vestal was Mr. Carpenter's secretary during the 1950s and she remembered Clyde Parker seventy-two years later! She recalled he started as a substitute teacher in 1951, and kept progressing as he earned degrees from UNCG and Duke. In **2022**, Norma with her husband were living in one of the apartments at Providence Place in High Point, where I also lived. She was sooo thrilled when she discovered I was writing a book about my life

as Clyde Parker's wife. Norma and her husband remembered what an outstanding teacher and pastor Clyde was while living in Elkin so many decades earlier.

Raymond Hanks was one of the Supervisors at the Chatham Blanket Mill in Elkin, owned by the Chatham family, the biggest employer in Elkin, at that time! Raymond's wife, Pete (Plutinee was her name), worked in the Mill office. She became one of the most loved people, directing and helping with all kinds of projects in the community and church. She organized and helped pull off the most unbelievable stunt with the **"Clyde Parker, This Is Your Life"** program.

There were so many people involved from around North Carolina, other states and one friend even flew in from California. The fact that Clyde Parker was completely surprised, was an accomplishment of considerable magnitude. While he was doing his usual Sunday afternoon visitations, people were arriving at the church. By the time he came home, the parking lot and the street were both filled with cars.

Beginning with Roy and Gladys Parker and his brother, Gerald, the script progressed through his life including his friend, Reese Allred, who had flown in for the program from California. Reece was Clyde's teenage friend who sometimes traveled with him during his early teen years of preaching. It was an unbelievable class act production that included the Mayor, and the Principals of North Elkin Elementary and Elkin High School, both schools in which he had taught!

We had only one car during those years and if I needed the car during the day, I would take Clyde to school, then go get him when school was over. We would then eat supper, and he would be gone the rest of the evening visiting in the hospital or in the community doing his pastoral duties. He was a very busy and very happy bi-vocational pastor/teacher/father/husband.

I vividly remember a warm Spring day I was on my way to pick up Clyde after school, and I was getting sleepier and… s l e e p i e r and then dropped off to sleep. The car drifted left, crossing the on coming lane and into the ditch across the road, but no one was coming.

I woke up in the ditch with dirt covering the car and filling the air like a cloud around me. I sat there trying to figure out what had happened. A truck coming toward me stopped and the driver got out to see if I was hurt. Thank the Lord I wasn't, so he directed me how to drive out of the ditch.

IF I had gone off the road a few feet earlier, I would have gone into a lake. IF I had gone off the road a few feet further, I would have gone down a deep ravine. The car didn't even have scratches on the side that hit the soft bank of dirt. I couldn't believe there were no rocks in the dirt!! It was clear to all: the Lord had directed this sleepy mother to the safest place to run off the road, and **I thanked Him!!**

One sunny, Spring Sunday, before the new church was built, Clyde scheduled a baptism service in a farm pond. The water was muddy and cow's footprints were all around as well as their "patties". Clyde and those to be baptized went into the muddy water. One of the men was rather heavy and Clyde put his left arm around his shoulders, his right hand over the man's mouth, his fingers pinching the man's nose shut.

Clyde started his comments and as he talked, the man was VERY badly needing to breathe. By the time Clyde was putting him under the water, they both lost their footing in the deep mud and you can imagine what happened. They both went down, and I thought they would, both, drown in that muddy water. Clyde didn't realize the man was just struggling to breathe! What a muddy mess they were! No one laughed then, but we sure laughed later, remembering the scary scene.

The man being baptized, was one of the many men who helped build the beautiful, new church building with a baptistery. It took a couple years to complete the new church because most of the work was done with volunteer labor. Skilled men gave their time in the evenings and on Saturdays....a wonderful testimony of loving service to the Lord.

Clyde's Grandpa Willie Parker outlived two wives. As he was nearing his 80th birthday, he asked a widow in the Richfield community to marry him, and asked his grandson, Clyde to perform the marriage ceremony, which was Clyde's first after he was ordained. Family and friends enjoyed that happy day on the porch of Grandpa Willie's farm house at the end of the road. Grandpa Willie had given acreage, not far from his home, for a Baptist church to build a church, which they named Parker Memorial Baptist Church, and that is where he was married.

Our first two children were at their Great-Grandpa Willie's marriage! Ronnie was three and Kenneth was a two-months old baby in a dress, in my arms! Back then, we put dresses on both little boys and girl babies until they were several months old.

I remember Grandpa Roy Phillips telling us that little boys wore dresses, in the early 1900s until they went to school. They had one pair of pants they wore to church or to town. There were no disposable diapers and they didn't buy cloth diapers. The toddlers could just pull up their dress and relieve themselves with no problems! For tiny new babies, Mamas would tear rags into squares or cut up old clothes into diapers.

When Ronnie was just a little boy, Clyde needed to run some errands so he took Ronnie with him. In one store, Clyde asked

Ronnie what he wanted, and he answered, *"I don't want anything."* Clyde insisted he wanted to buy him something. Ronnie finally said, *"Daddy I don't want anything. I just want to be with you."*

Clyde's heart melted with love for his little boy....who had just delivered a **powerful** message to him! From then on Clyde started taking his little boys, individually, or together when running errands or visiting with parishioners.

Kenneth remembered being taken on some of his Dad's summer trips to Duke University for classes. He remembered being inspired to also keep going to school to earn a doctorate when he got older!

As the children became teenagers, Clyde took each one, individually, on long trips. Little Ronnie's simple message of **"wanting to be with Daddy"** became Clyde's passion to fulfill, which he did many times, taking them, individually, on trips across the United States or to other countries over seas.

One of our trips to California was with G'pa and G'ma Phillips when my brother and sister, Wesley and Marietta were little children and our Ronnie Sr. was a little boy,... seven of us in G'pa's BIG Buick. Since there were several drivers, we traveled 24 hours a day, going across the United States in record time!! One night Clyde was driving and SUDDENLY he screeched to a stop, waking us all. He just gasped, pointing to a HUGE jack rabbit poised to jump into the road. Then he and we realized it was a billboard cut to look like a jack rabbit, advertising a restaurant called "Jack Rabbit". Silhouetted against the night desert sky, it did look like a BIG desert jack rabbit we had been mentally picturing, in some of the stories G'pa Phillips had been telling us!!!!!

In Elkin, there was a pastor at the Presbyterian Church who resembled Clyde, and drove the same kind of car, a Volkswagen "beetle". It was no wonder the people in Elkin got them mixed up and called each by the other's name sometimes. One day Ronnie and

Kenneth were in the car with me, and started yelling "Daddy" at the car in front of us, but it was the "other" pastor! It was sooo funny!

After lunch one day, the boys and I picked Clyde up at school. His principal, Mr. Rogers, had given him permission to leave early to attend a District Board Meeting and then preach in a revival that night. We were on Center Road in the country when Clyde realized he had left his briefcase with his sermon in it at home. He stopped the car and told me to go back home and get his briefcase. *"I'll get out and walk in these woods until you get back. I can't go back through town. I'm afraid Mr. Carpenter will see me and he wouldn't like it that Mr. Rogers gave me permission to leave early."*

When we returned thirty minutes later, I blew the horn and he came out of the woods and got into the car. *"Don't ever tell anyone what a silly thing I did. What would people think if they saw me in the woods dressed in a suit and then get into the car with you"*. As I thought about it I just couldn't resist the temptation to play a joke on him. So, with the help of Raymond Hanks and his wife, "Miss Pete", we set the scene for the joke pretending that Raymond had "heard something".

One day when we four were together, Raymond asked, *"What kind of person is the Presbyterian pastor?"* Clyde assured him that the preacher was a fine man. *"Well a strange thing happened a few weeks ago. My friend was filling a fuel tank in a tobacco barn on Center road and he saw that Presbyterian preacher in the woods. He watched and a woman came along and picked him up. We just wondered if he was a good and honest man."*

Poor Clyde told Raymond to tell that fuel truck driver you can't always believe what you **think** you see. Finally Clyde knew he couldn't let the Presbyterian preacher's reputation be ruined because of him....so he told Raymond the whole story, **that it was**

him. Raymond, Miss Pete and I laughed and laughed,.... But for some reason Clyde didn't think it was funny at all!!

Chapter 17
Color Blind

In the mid 1950s when Clyde was teaching at North Elkin Elementary School, he would drive past a little one-room, old school building where the black children of Elkin attended in the first through eighth grades. I remember he stopped one day to meet and talk with the black teacher who was teaching all eight grades in the one classroom. He came home stunned and angry about how very unfair and unChristian the educational system was.

His desire and drive to further his own education, and his color blindness compelled him to enroll in Summer School classes at the all black Central College in Raleigh in the late 1950s. I remember one day his teacher called, telling him the racial tensions in Raleigh were so high that, in his best interest, he should not come to class. He had never mentioned to me any animosity he felt from fellow students or teachers.

He continued taking Saturday classes at the University of North Carolina in Greensboro. Following graduation with a Masters in Education, he continued Saturday and Summer classes at Duke to earn a Doctorate in Education. All his educational pursuits were while he was ALSO in three building programs at the Elkin Pilgrim Church. The congregation had also grown from a couple dozen people to over a couple hundred.

Clyde Parker: Pastor; University Professor; Businessman

In the Fall of 1966 the Trustees of Southern Pilgrim College (SPC) in Kernersville, N.C. gave him a call to be President. Since he was now highly qualified, with his doctorate degree from Duke University, they wanted him to help them become accredited with the Association of Christian Colleges. With the approval of the S.P.C. Trustees, he also became a teacher at Bennett College in Greensboro, with an all black student body of girls.

With his call to preach and desire to be a pastor, Clyde was most unhappy being President of Southern Pilgrim College, so he asked the District Superintendent to find him a church to pastor. Rev. Adrain Grout, pastor of First Pilgrim Church in High Point, had suffered a stroke. Pastor Grout was asking the Lord for healing and was determined to stay as pastor, so the church gave Clyde a call to come be Rev. Grout's Associate Pastor.

Clyde also gained permission from the church trustees to teach at Winston Salem State University. WSSU had been an all black university since its historic beginning, and Clyde became their first full-time white professor. "Color-blind" Clyde was so loved by students and colleagues, he was awarded the honor of "professor of the year", twice during his fourteen years teaching there.

While on the WSSU faculty, Clyde went to heaven from the plane crash. The Chancellor and the head of the Education Department, asked the family to allow them to speak a few words at Clyde's Memorial Service. Their warm comments confirmed what everyone present knew! Clyde was a "color-blind" pastor and teacher. The next week, Winston Salem State University had a Memorial Service for Clyde Parker in their large auditorium, which was filled with students and faculty. He was a much loved professor.

Chapter 18
Clyde's Third Track– Business Man

Our oldest son, Ronnie Sr, was his Daddy's right hand man, so this chapter is what **his** keen mind remembers from decades ago when his Daddy, Clyde, began and continued his "business life". Ronnie **drove** many thousands of miles, and, also, **flew** thousands more miles, going **anywhere** his Dad needed him to go, thanks to his patient wife, Beverly. I have no memory of Beverly ever complaining of her husband's sometimes extensive days of traveling, even though their children were preteen age children. Bev was the librarian in an Elementary Winston Salem City School.

Clyde and I realized then and knew for sure, as the years went by, that God had orchestrated Ronnie's marriage to Beverly Beach, after they met as high school students at Kernersville Wesleyan Academy. Her incredible parents, Rev and Mrs. Charles Beach, were pastors in the Washington D.C. area. With Bev's encouragement and keen mind, she and Ronnie Sr. have worked together through the decades. Ronnie was, and still is, an incredibly wise man, and with brilliant Beverly by his side, their love for the Lord and Kingdom building is their **passion.**

Clyde's third track of achievements started out as a hobby or diversion from pastoring and teaching. Our dentist in Elkin, Dr. Fox, asked Clyde if he wanted to buy three small four-room rental houses beside the parsonage. Clyde told him he didn't have the money to buy them, so Dr. Fox said he would finance the project, which he did.

The rest of this chapter is what Ronnie Sr, remembered:

Daddy thought he had financing lined up to buy a small office building in Winston Salem, and was preparing to close. In the process, the lender changed the terms requiring him to have equity that he did not have. Daddy became distraught, worrying more about his reputation for committing to buy something he couldn't afford, than actually owning the property. The lender finally loaned him the money they had originally agreed upon.

When the nursing home industry was in its infancy in the early 1970s, Daddy was approached by a man who offered to manage a nursing home if Daddy would help him get the financing. That first facility was in Charlotte, NC. Daddy was able to negotiate the loan for that facility. Over the course of about ten years, he was able to acquire the financing and equity needs through first and second mortgage loans to include facilities in Kentucky, Mississippi, Arkansas, Tennessee as well as more in North Carolina.

Daddy was also able to take those skills to help First Wesleyan Church achieve the "cradle to the grave" ministries he had envisioned for the church. When he arrived in 1968 as Associate Pastor, the 400 plus congregation had Sunday morning and evening services and a Wednesday evening prayer service. There were three employees, Pastor Grout, his secretary, and the janitor. Within the year, Daddy encouraged Pastor Grout to enlarge the pastoral staff which he did.

By 1984, when Daddy went to heaven, the Day Care facility for children was the largest in the state of North Carolina. By 2020, on the North side of the church, the Elementary, Middle and High

School facilities had over a thousand students, one of the largest Christian schools in North Carolina

The acreage on the south side of the church included a skilled nursing facility, personal care facility and independent retirement living apartments. The value of all the facilities at the time of Daddy's death was over $20,000,000 with approximately $3,000,000 indebtedness.

When he envisioned this expansion of ministry, Daddy never once called on the church to contribute anything. His business plan and execution were to see that these ministries be self-supporting and self-sustaining. In fact, the continual growth of the church membership was enabled by using the school classrooms which were not used on weekends. The school graciously provided the school classrooms to be used on Sunday as Sunday School classes, for a nominal custodial charge each week

Chapter 19
Clyde's Overseas Travels

In the Summer of 1960, when Ronnie was nine, Kenneth four and Phyllis one, Clyde made his first overseas trip with teenager, Larry Hanks. For **eight weeks**, their well planned trip took them to the Holy Land, Asia, and several European countries as well as some African countries. Raymond and Pete Hanks teenage son, Larry, was an excellent traveling companion on that long, energy sapping trip.

This is a copy of the letter Clyde sent to be read to the annual District Conference delegates:

> *"Greetings to the North Carolina Conference of the Pilgrim Holiness Church: I write you with mixed emotions. First I am very thankful for the opportunity of visiting the Holy Land to see the places Jesus walked and taught, while on earth. Second, I feel just a bit sad when I think this is the first Conference I will have missed since age thirteen. I have attended fifteen consecutive Annual Conferences.*
>
> *I pray God's blessings on you, my brothers and sisters in the Lord and trust this will be the greatest Conference for the sake of the Kingdom of Heaven in the history of the Conference.*

By the time this message reaches you, we will be among the natives of Northern Rhodesia. I will give Miss Thompson, Miss Wagoner and Miss Scott your regards and express your concern for their best in God's work."

*Your Brother in Christ,
Clyde A. Parker*

Miss Thompson, Miss Wagoner and Miss Scott, missionary teachers in North Rhodesia, good friends of ours, were all three from the North Carolina Conference of the Pilgrim Holiness Church.

After that successful two month's overseas trip, the travel agent suggested that Clyde should take groups of people to the Holy Land. During the 1960s, 1970s and early 1980s, Clyde took groups of people between Christmas and the first week of January to the Holy Land. A few times there were over 100 people and once there were more than 200. Most of the trips, however, were with 50 or more people. Clyde was an excellent organizer and people were happy to travel with him.

I remember on one trip while we were in Hebron to see Abraham and Sarah's tomb, a terrorist with a hand grenade suddenly got into our group. Soldiers very quickly grabbed him, but he wrestled out of their hands, his coat falling just a few feet from me. Soldiers followed him around the building and down the alley where they shot him, but it was scary. When it was over, I suddenly realized Phyllis, who was about eight years old, was squeezed between me and the rock wall behind me.

One of our Summer trips was to Haiti to attend the Clyde Dupin Crusade where thousands and thousands of Haitians attended the outdoor stadium when hundreds went forward to receive Christ as their Savior. We also took a side trip to LaGanauve Island to visit the Wesleyan School and Hospital. Returning to the mainland, our little motorboat was in a storm with waves taking us high in the air, then going so low we were beneath the ocean level…UP and down we went! Clyde went to sleep, but I was sooo frightened, I finally had to wake him up to help me not be so frightened. As I've said before, Clyde Parker was a **most unusual** man!!

Chapter 20
Tough–But Happy Times

AN EMOTIONALLY SHATTERING event was when I was in the Elkin hospital delivering our fourth child. Dr. McNeill, for some strange reason, THOUGHT he was hearing two heart beats. At that time, there were no sonograms at the Elkin Hospital, so he told Clyde it appeared he was having twins! At that time, the Daddy was not allowed in the delivery room, so Clyde paced back and forth in the waiting room. After a very difficult delivery, Dr. McNeill helped ten pound Clyde Jr. take his first breath of air and his Daddy breathed a BIG sigh of relief! We were so happy our last three children were born in Elkin.

Clyde had told me if this baby is a boy, he wanted us to name him Clyde, Jr. **"I want a son to bear my name."** Clyde Jr. graduated from Taylor University, where our Youth Pastor, Rev. Mark Welch has graduated. Coming back home, he married Kim who had been one of his classmates in **Kindergarten in 1971**, the beginning year of First Wesleyan Church's Wesleyan Christian Academy.

When Kim realized he wanted to be a lawyer, after he had become a CPA, she encouraged him to go to Wake Forest Law School while she taught at Wesleyan Christian Academy. He became a successful lawyer carrying forward his Dad's committed Christian legacy! With Kim by his side, their two daughters, Sydney and Shelby finished college with master's degrees and have professional occupations.

An emotionally shattering event for me was finding a copperhead snake in the living room platform rocker. We gingerly carried the chair out the door and into the yard where Clyde Sr. was able to find and kill the poisonous snake. However, my fear that there might be more in the house grew in such intensity that I became emotionally paralyzed. Clyde was exasperated with me, as I was with myself.

The next day after he left for school, I cried out to the Lord for help. He seemed to direct my thought that if God can heal bodies instantly from diseases and brokenness, surely He could heal my crippling mental condition. Within the next few seconds after I verbalized my hearts desire for healing of this mental fear... it happened!. It was like a cleansing from my head to my feet, and the fear was completely gone! It was as if a ball and chain had been cut loose from me. I walked through the house, with no fear of seeing a snake... weeping for joy. That is a wonderful memory of "mental" healing.

One Summer Saturday, Clyde said, *"Let's paint the dining room and living rooms."* Any wife is happy for her husband to be so helpful and have such a positive, cheerful suggestion. That's true, unless you are having out of town company for supper...and we were. No amount of begging or explaining could steer him off his determination that it **could** be done! I pulled down curtains and started washing windows while he painted. Would you believe both rooms were painted, supper was cooking on the stove and I had just hung the last curtain when company pulled into the driveway. They would never have known if they couldn't smell the new paint, so I shared with them the whole day's events!

While we were in Elkin, Clyde not only was pastoring and teaching school, he was traveling to UNCG earning his Masters degree in Education. As soon as he graduated, he tried to enroll at

Duke University, but his undergrad transcript showed what a poor student he had been, so they refused to accept him as a student. One of his friends, whose last name was Bryson, was enrolled as a doctoral student and he went with Clyde to the Graduate office. Together they successfully convinced the registrant that Clyde was a different student than he was in college and they accepted him into the Doctoral program.

He had Saturday classes as well as Summer classes. He would **study** with his notes or book on the steering wheel as he drove back and forth from Elkin to Durham. I thanked the Lord many times for protecting him from accidents during those days. Any time we made trips together, I read to him and questioned him from notes he had taken in classes.

During his senior year, his dissertation was titled, "The Legality of the Use of Public School Facilities by Non School Groups." With my help, we surveyed many public school systems scattered all over the United States and discovered that with very few exceptions, churches could meet in school facilities.

There have been many changes over the past eight decades that have mandated public school teachers and principals cannot refer to Biblical principles or encourage christian students. When I was an elementary school student in the Salisbury, NC **public school** in the late 1930s, early 1940s, each day was started with students taking turns reading from the Bible and praying our simple prayers, or The Lord's Prayer. What drastic changes the decades have brought with mandates that no references to the Bible may be made and certainly no praying in the public school classroom. Because of this, there has been a proliferation of Private and Christian Schools in America.

Chapter 21
Two Years At Kernersville Pilgrim Bible College

After Clyde earned a Doctorate in Educational Administration from Duke University, the Board of Trustees of the North Carolina District of Pilgrim Churches, put pressure on Clyde to accept the position as President of Pilgrim Bible College, a combination High School, Junior College and Bible College.

In July, 1967 we said goodby to fourteen years of memories with our beloved Elkin congregation and moved to Kernersville with our little family of four children: Ronnie Sr. was sixteen, Kenneth twelve, Phyllis, eight and Clyde Jr. was eight months old.

The School Board agreed to allow Clyde to teach at Bennett College, a Methodist College in Greensboro for black girls. His teaching schedule allowed him the flexibility to do both jobs well. He endeared himself to the students and faculty at Bennett during those late 1960s when race relations were at a flash point. There were a few days he was advised to not come on campus for his safety because of the riots on the nearby AT&T campus. He never expressed feeling any animosity during the two years he taught there.

Clyde's primary responsibility at Kernersville Pilgrim College, after administration, was to raise money for the school by traveling each weekend to churches with the Choir or Singing Ensemble.

Being a pastor at heart and calling, he was miserable for the two years we were in Kernersville. I was totally immersed in mothering and studying. Living on the campus and having plenty of babysitters for Clyde Jr, I submitted to Clyde's **insistence** that I get a college degree! I enrolled and began my first year of college, taking fifteen and sometimes eighteen hours of classes each semester. Sometimes in cold weather I would study outside, bundled against the cold in order to stay awake and alert to read. It was an interesting and challenging time for me also.

Clyde asked the District Superintendent to please find a church for him to pastor, with the threat that if he couldn't find anything for him, he would look into another denomination. In order to have a "bird in hand" he called the United Methodist District Superintendent in eastern North Carolina and also applied for a teaching job at Pembroke University, where his brother, Gerald, was offered a job as a professor in the School of Education.

Both places confirmed they had openings for him to work. However, events were beginning to take place that eventually led him to be Associate Pastor at First Wesleyan Church in High Point.

Chapter 22
Plant "Prayer Seeds" Early in Life

CLYDE SR HAD introduced his teenage son, Ronnie Sr., to the game of golf even though he seldom ever took that much time away from his many ministry responsibilities. Actually he didn't really enjoy playing golf,... but to spend quality time with his young son, he took him to play golf.

Years later, Ronnie Sr was golfing with his young grandson, Stephen, and there was the sound of a siren going down the road. They couldn't see if it was an ambulance or fire truck, but Stephen said to his granddad, *"we need to pray"*. He folded his hands, bowed his head and they prayed for whoever was hurting or in trouble. It made no difference to Stephen if other golfers were near by, they needed to pray!

When Shelby was a very little girl, she and Kim were outside their home talking with a neighbor. The sound of a siren went down the street and Shelby tugged at Kim's hand saying, *"pay, Mommie pay."* Kim explained to the neighbor that they always pray when they hear a siren. She stooped down beside little Shelby, whose hands were folded, and they prayed for whoever was hurting or in trouble.

There's another story about the power of prayer that turned a very disobedient dog around. In High Point we had a feisty white poodle named Marty. Rosa was ironing for me one day when Roy

Rummage, a pastor friend of ours, knocked on the back door. Rosa opened the door, and quick as a flash, Marty was out the door running full speed across the field where Wesleyan Christian Academy now stands.

Rosa called, but the dog ran faster and was disappearing from view. Frantically, Rosa prayed, pointing to the dog, ***"In the name of Jesus Christ you come back here."*** She said the dog made a U-turn and came running back as fast as he had left with his ears laid back. He came whooshing past her into the kitchen as if he were being chased by something. Our preacher friend was totally amazed at such a quick answer to prayer! Rosa was a sweet christian black lady who believed God meant what He promised in Philippians 4:6.

Chapter 23
From Elkin to High Point

In 1968, the General Conferences of the Pilgrim Holiness Churches and the Wesleyan Methodist Churches, voted to merge the denominations into one, and name it The Wesleyan Church. It so happened Clyde was a delegate to that General Conference in Anderson, Indiana. What a thrilling event it was for delegates in each merging denomination.

Looking back from this point in time, it is easy to see that the Lord had prepared Clyde, long before he was called to High Point 1st Wesleyan church in 1967, to be the catalyst for inspiring the church leadership to start a school and nursing and retirement communities.

The church leadership realized they needed to call an Assistant Pastor to help Dr. Adrain Grout after he had a stroke. Rev. R.S. Shelton, District Superintendent recommended Clyde Parker who had proven his ability to pastor as well as teach on the college level. The church board recommended him and the church membership voted,... but there were so many "NO" votes, he couldn't go.

In the fourteen years he had pastored in Elkin, he had not received any "no" votes. The overwhelming negative **"we don't want Clyde Parker"** was so baffling, he was crushed emotionally. He had preached in that church several times when he was a teenager. He called his brother Gerald, who was a professor at Pembroke

University in east Carolina, and discovered they were looking for a professor in their Education Department.

Clyde also contacted the District Superintendent of the United Methodist churches in eastern North Carolina to see if they needed a pastor. The D.S. responded with a "yes" and gave him an invitation to come pastor one of their churches, near Pembroke University.

Clyde called Superintendent Shelton to tell him he was going to leave the Wesleyan denomination, and would he please let the High Point First Church board know he was not available.

Three of the church Board of Trustees members, who were professionals in their field of work, contacted the General Board members of the Wesleyan denomination in Indianapolis, asking for permission to have a **second** vote. When they were granted permission, the Board members of First Wesleyan, began laboriously making personal contact with the members of the church. They went into detail explaining Clyde Parker's unique Pastoral achievements and Educational credentials. They also let the membership know, they had permission to have a second vote.

Very reluctantly, Clyde gave the church board permission to run his name again, but he also explained he would not promise to accept a call, **unless** the Lord **strongly** let him know HE wanted him to go to High Point First Wesleyan Church. The church did have another election and there were still quite a few "no" votes, but not enough to prevent Clyde from accepting the call. After much prayer, the Lord strongly impressed him to accept the call and go as Dr. Grout's Assistant Pastor.

In 1968 when we moved to High Point, the North Carolina State Educational System had mandated integration of all schools, from Elementary Schools to Universities. At that point in time, the State University system had several colleges and a couple universities for African American students. Winston Salem State University, for black students, asked Clyde to come as a **tenured Full Professor**. That rarely ever happened, if ever, but in God's plan, WSSU was delighted to get a white professor, who loved black people, and had a doctorate from Duke University! Teaching and supervising student teachers at WSSU gave Clyde the idea and inspiration to start a quality christian school at 1st Wesleyan that would be integrated.

In 1968, the acreage to the south of the church was a farm including a big farm house with farm equipment in the yard. The land was offered for sale, but the church board felt they couldn't buy it, so John Lain and Clyde tied it up with personally borrowed money until the church could buy it.

Concurrently, a friend had asked Clyde to be his business partner investing in a nursing home in Gastonia and then one in Charlotte. Because of that exciting experience in health care, Clyde, individually planted the seed thought with the church leadership. They caught the vision of starting the retirement community and nursing facility on the acreage beside the church. Rev. James Denny, who had been Clyde's long time friend, from Marion College days, was called to come supervise the building of the facilities and be the Administrator of the Retirement Community and Nursing facility.

Rev. Denny's astute business background and sterling leadership ability encouraged a conventional church to accept unconventional challenges. Within twelve years, three hundred employees were required to staff ministries that included a hundred-bed Nursing Home, a hundred-bed Rest Home, two hundred Apartments in the retirement community, a Day Care for preschool children, Elementary School, High School, a Counseling Center, Printing and Transportation facilities, all sprawling over 38 acres.

Dr. Grout, Senior Pastor for 34 years, welcomed and encouraged Clyde Parker and James Denny in the development of the Retirement Community on one side and the School on the other side of the church. They worked together as a father and sons. When Dr. Grout retired, Clyde became senior pastor. James Denny moved across the driveway, from his Wesleyan Arms office, and became Clyde's Associate Pastor.

The interchange and life-enriching influences that flowed between the Retirement Community and the Academy students seemed limitless. A retired college basketball coach watched, from his wheelchair, as the basketball team practiced and played other teams in the Academy Gym. You could see it at the Swimming Pool as the Aquatics Director taught the octogenarians to swim or just enjoy water exercise. It was evident in the mutual love between the youngsters and oldsters in the Nursing Home rooms through the Academy's Adopt-a-Grandparent program.

Clyde Parker had dreamed of a school where loving Christian teachers could see and nurture the potential of each child, regardless of innate ability. His dream was realized at Wesleyan Christian Academy.

Clyde's eighth grade teacher, in 1944, failed to factor in drive and determination with Clyde's apparent lack of academic ability, and she drew the wrong conclusions. In 1983, her boss, the Superintendent of Kannapolis City Schools retired to the Wesleyan Arms Retirement community of senior citizens whose lives were enriched by Wesleyan Christian Academy. Both were dreams of Clyde Parker, an academic underachiever,... according to his eighth grade teacher's estimation.

The church leadership allowed Clyde to continue teaching at WSSU full time the fifteen years he was pastor. He had the uncanny ability to inspire and trust the administrators of the various church ministries to do their jobs **without** his supervision. It appeared his Doctorate in Educational Administration had taught him to delegate and release control so he could do his primary job of pastoring.

Chapter 24
More High Point Memories

IN THE EARLY 1970s 1st Wesleyan church had voted to put the school building behind the church, and the plans were already being drawn. One night Clyde sat straight up in bed and said out loud, *"That's right we can't put the school there"*. Startled awake, I didn't know what was going on. *"What are you talking about?"* I asked. *"We can't put the school behind the church, it would not be seen and we would have no place to grow"*, he said.

One by one he started talking individually to the school board members sharing what he felt the Lord had shown him. At the next board meeting, they were all in agreement it should be built beside the church. The beautiful Wesleyan Academy buildings and campus have grown just as Pepaw Clyde saw it that night many decades ago.

The Lord had gifted Clyde to be a very wise pastor. He didn't TELL people what to do. He had the gift of leadership and would give reasons WHY doing something was a good idea. He could then back away and let someone else take credit for an idea. **That made Clyde Parker a good leader.**

Clyde's doctorate in educational administration from Duke University only validated the wonderful gift of leadership the Lord had given him. There are many examples of that gift of leadership through the decades of constant building programs at 1st Wesleyan church campus on North Centennial Street.

During those fifteen years something was always under construction at the school, church, or retirement community consisting of a nursing home, assisted living facility, free standing apartments and a HUD apartment building. James Denny, the Retirement Center Administrator, and Clyde Parker worked like a hand in a glove under the direction of their heavenly Father to Whom they both listened and obeyed!!

One day driving home from his teaching job at Winston Salem State University, Clyde realized his date book was lost or misplaced. That was a very serious loss, because his appointments were now lost as well as his visitation records. After searching his office at the University his Christian secretary from Jamaica knelt by her chair and prayed for Clyde to find it.

Back home he searched his church office, then came to the house and we both searched through the house and the car. We retraced our steps, looking everywhere again. It was crucial or him to find that lost book, so we prayed again asking God to help us find it.

Clyde went back to the church office and I went back to the car to search again. I opened the door, and there on the front seat **in plain sight** was Clyde's lost date book!! **It couldn't be true, but there it was.** There is no logical explanation. God must have dispatched an angel to recover that lost book to help Clyde! It was NOT on the front seat while Clyde drove home from the university, it was NOT on the front seat when we searched the car twice. We thanked his Godly University secretary for her prayer to find the book and she rejoiced with us in God's awesome miraculous answer to prayer

When Ronnie and Kenneth were little boys, we gave away their feisty little dog to a family that lived a couple hours away from High Point. The boys were heart broken and we felt badly about it. I honestly can't remember WHY we gave the dog away, but there must have been a good reason. Neither do I recall how long it was before that dog showed up at our house.

That dog was smart enough to travel seventy-five or more miles to find us again, because the boys might have remained upset with us. The dog and boys were very happy, but I don't know how happy the family was that we gave it to. The miracles of sustaining and surviving life in the plant and animal world make it easy to believe in the God who created the universe and everything in it.

In the 1970s Clyde and I saw a little "chapel on wheels" in Greensboro that was used as the Child Evangelism Chapel that went to state and county fairs. The teachers taught children about Jesus with Bible stories and songs. BINGO! A thought exploded in our heads. We need to get a children's chapel for our church.

Clyde drew plans and gave them to a mobile trailer builder near Salisbury. He designed it with long narrow windows, a door on the side, a door on the back with a small porch, and a steeple on the roof. It really DID look like a miniature church! We had an old van to pull it around High Point to various locations with teams of people developing their own "stops".

First we would visit the homes in the community, so the parents knew who we were and would let their children come. Hundreds and hundreds of little and big children heard about Jesus as they attended the little "chapel on wheels".

Years later, I was walking down the street, and an African American man coming toward me started smiling. Pointing to himself and then me, his arms went around me, as he started singing, *"I love you and you love me, His banner over us is love...."* The little song he had learned in the Mobile Chapel, years before, is based on one of the names of Jesus: Jehovah Nissi. Read the story in Exodus 17:8-16.

Clyde and I flew to Florida with John Storey in his little four-seater purple airplane as he was taking his daughter, Starr to the

Florida Bowl ball game for her birthday present. We rented the last car available at the airport and took them to the ball park, then drove to Disneyland where Phyllis and Rick were singing with the ReGeneration, The Glory and Majesty of Christmas, for their Nativity Pageant.

At the gate, we were told we were at the wrong place. The Pageant was at the Buena Vista Outdoor Theater. Back on the busy road we finally found it but it was now time for the show, with people standing at the fence, looking in. Clyde asked the lady at the gate where the Victorian Singers would enter and she said, *"right here"*.

Phyllis and Rick didn't even know we were there, and we would have to leave for the airport as soon as the show was over, so Clyde asked the gate lady if she would give Phyllis a note from us. *"Why don't you go right now to their dressing room...but you must hurry"*, she said, showing us where to go.

As we ran in that direction, they were shocked to see us. There was only a minute to talk as Phyllis introduced us to the producer, explaining we had just arrived. *"Do you have seats?"* she asked. *"Oh no, we will just stand at the fence and listen,"* we replied. "**Follow me,**" she said with authority. When we hesitated, Phyllis' hand pushed us!!

She told the gate lady, *"they are with me,"* and we followed her all the way to the front seats where she pulled "RESERVED" signs off two chairs and told us to sit! We enjoyed the show from the best seats in the amphitheater as we silently thanked the Lord over and over.

There is a Bible verse in Psalm 139 that says God has every day of our lives planned. God perfectly timed our steps that day: we got the last rental car at the airport; went to Disneyland first, but found Buena Vista just in time; the Gate lady gave us directions; the producer took us to the front seats. God had taken care of us better than we could have ever PLANNED the day ourselves, AND we found Starr and her Dad on time

Rick and Phyllis traveled and sang with Derric Johnson's Re'Generation Singers for almost five years, performing approximately 500 times a year in Concerts, Conventions, Conferences, Civic and Political Gatherings. They were home only two weeks during each year.

Performing as the Victorian Singers at the Disney Nativity had become an annual event. When Disney World owned EPCOT, Derric Johnson became their Music Consultant and the Re'Generation Singers became the Voices of Liberty at the American Pavilion.

During the five years Phyllis traveled and sang with ReGeneration, she got sick one day and their leader, Derric Johnson called us to come get her. After church on a Sunday night, Clyde flew in his little airplane to get her. The airport, on the top of a hill in Parkersburg, West Virginia, had been leveled off. Clyde told me later, *"Landing on that mountain top at night was scary."*

The doctor said she had mononucleosis and needed complete bed rest, only getting up to go to the bathroom and to eat. After a week at home, the doctor said she could join the group again, BUT only to sing, eat and go to the bathroom. So, she slept for two weeks all day in the sleeper of the diesel truck cab. She barely had strength to sing and then back to the sleeper she would go.

The ReGeneration traveled in three cars and two trucks with lots of lights, sound and sight equipment, plus the group's many costumes. Big pictures were shown on screens as they sang. They sang in every state except Hawaii and Alaska. God miraculously protected them during those years with no accidents or tragedies on the road.

Another blessing, for us, was that Rick Webb was in the group and he fell in love with Phyllis. They got married at 1st Wesleyan in

Clyde Parker: Pastor; University Professor; Businessman

High Point in 1982 with the sanctuary and balcony filled with their many friends. Years later, Parker and Hannah, two of their children, sang with them as a family for decades, making friends all over the United States as well as several countries of the world.

Clyde and I flew to Coldwater, Michigan for our Youth Pastor, Mark Welch's wedding to Lori on a Saturday evening. Early Sunday morning there was a cold rain covering everything with a coat of ice. What else did we expect to have in Coldwater!!

We went to church and after lunch we proceeded to the airport where Clyde knocked ice off the wings and we flew away. We were in clouds, sometimes so thick I couldn't see the ends of the plane wings. Clyde was instrument rated which meant he knew how to fly looking only at his instruments. I had memorized I Corinthians 10:13, *"He will not let you be tempted beyond what you can bear. But when you are tempted, He will also provide a way to escape that you may be able to bear it."*

I kept talking to the Lord about my temptation to FEAR... to be REALLY AFRAID! I asked Him to let me faint if we were going to crash, since that would be my way to escape. I didn't faint and we finally arrived at the Greensboro airport. However, the fog was as low as the tree tops, and the buzzer sounded that we were at the end of the runway, but we couldn't SEE it. Clyde turned the plane up and we went back into the thick cloud.

The tower vectored us back around and I still had not fainted. In fact the tower talked us back to the end of the runway, but we still could not see anything but clouds. *"You are now over the runway, PUT–IT–**DOWN**,"* the controller sternly said. Clyde kept his eyes on the instruments and we popped through the fog and there we were ON THE RUNWAY! **WHEW!!** Clyde was so wise to keep his eyes on the instruments and we were safely on the ground.

"*Thank You, Jesus*," I wept!! Clyde loved to fly and that trip certainly was a test of his skill as an instrument pilot!!

When we were doing Evangelism Explosion at 1st Wesleyan, Clyde and I flew to Fort Lauderdale, Florida, in the little airplane, for an EE Conference at the Coral Ridge Presbyterian Church. In groups of three, we went out in the evenings to ask people if they knew Jesus. I was teamed with a lawyer from Coral Ridge Church and a man from Spain. Driving to the beach, our assigned place, I asked Marcos how he heard about Jesus and invited Him into his heart. He told us the most amazing answer to that question I've ever heard.

Back in Spain, his father was a famous matador, and was very angry with his son for not wanting to become a matador. The father walked away from him and his mother, and left them no money. They lived in a one-room apartment and his mother found just enough work for them to survive.

One day, two men knocked on their door to sell them a book. Marcos mother bought one for a few pennies. They read the book together, and discovered it was God's Word. At that time it was illegal to own a Bible in Spain.

Marcos' mother overheard two women in the market whispering about a Bible study in a home, and asked if she and Marcos could come. The women were shocked that Marcos and his mother had a Bible. When they heard the story of the illegal Bible salesmen, they were MORE shocked. NOBODY else had seen or heard of them. Attending the secret home Bible study, Marcos and his mother invited Jesus to live in their hearts.

When Marcos was a teenager he had to join the army. At the end of the training, there was a big celebration ceremony, requiring the new soldiers to bow down to a statue of the King of Spain. Thousands of people were at the ceremony, but, remembering the

Bible story to only bow to God, Marcos refused to bow to the statue of the King of Spain.

The military police took him to the General. Marcos told him the Bible story about the three Hebrew men, Shadrach, Meschach and Abednego who refused to bow to the King. They were thrown into the fiery furnace, but God saved them!! The General liked Marcos' courage and asked him to be his personal secretary during his time in the army.

I asked, *"Marcos, do you believe it's possible those Bible salesmen could have been angels?"* He answered, *"Oh, yes, my mother and I and our friends believe they were, because no one else saw them."* At the time I met Marcos he was the National Superintendent of a group of Protestant churches in Spain. The national law was also changed and it wasn't against the law to own a Bible.

On an early Saturday morning, actually before we even got out of bed, Clyde got a phone call that lasted probably an hour. To get more comfortable, he sat on the floor, leaning against the bed. I could sense that the person on the phone was being unkind to Clyde, but he was kind as he tried to explain his actions in a situation. The person on the phone was not listening to Clyde's explanation.

When the conversation finally ended he lay face down into the carpet and cried. I thought my heart would break. Clyde had been so misunderstood, I feared the hurt would never go away and he would have trouble being an effective pastor to this family. I knelt down beside him, gently massaging his back as I silently prayed: *"Lord, please heal the hurt to Clyde's spirit and mind so he can be a good pastor to this family."* Very quickly I thought, *"there are scars when wounds heal."* Then I remembered, *"but there are plastic surgeons who can take scars off the human body, so do I dare ask the Lord to do 'plastic surgery' on Clyde's memory?"* That is what I silently prayed for, that God would take away the scar of that hurtful phone call so he would never remember it!

Clyde got up from the floor took a shower and didn't talk about it that day, nor the next day, nor the next week, or the next month. He never mentioned it again and I never saw him being unkind to the person or to his family.

Oh dear, I'm such a curious kitten. About a year later, we were in the car, going on a trip, and I very carefully mentioned the incident. He looked at me funny and said *"I don't know what you are talking about, Ernie."* I said no more and he didn't ask, but in my heart I said, *"Thank You, Lord for doing plastic surgery to Clyde's memory!".*

In December 1983 I had a **disturbing dream** in which Clyde, Clyde Jr and I were sitting around the table eating dinner. All of a sudden Clyde started sliding down in his chair and his eyes rolled back. He would have fallen to the floor if Clyde Jr had not jumped up and caught him. His eyes closed and he couldn't talk. We carried him to the car and rushed him to the hospital. There was no 911 emergency call in the early 1980s. After a long time in the hospital emergency room, the doctor came out and told me that the circuits were overloaded in Clyde's brain.

I woke up about that time and Clyde was sleeping peacefully beside me. I told Wesley, my doctor brother, about my dream and he laughed saying he had never heard of any medical terms like that. The dream did make me start thinking about how busy Clyde was with SO MANY things to do and think about. I wanted to take better care of him, just in case his heart would get tired and stop beating, or his brain shut down. I found where I could take CPR training and went through the course.

About a month after my dream Clyde did go to heaven from the plane crash. It was a bad emergency, and no one could get him out of the plane. I was so glad Clyde had invited Jesus to live in his heart when he was just a little boy so Jesus took him to heaven from the burning airplane.

Chapter 25
January 30, 1984, Airplane Crash

JANUARY 30, 1984 started out a normal day. Ronnie Sr. brought Ronnie Jr. and Tammy by the parsonage very early before school time. They lived in Kernersville, but Beverly was the Librarian in a Winston Salem Middle School. Clyde and Ronnie Sr. had made plans to fly early to Wilmington and would be back by mid-afternoon.

When it was time for school, Ronnie Jr, Tammy and I stood at the back door to pray before they walked across the parsonage yard to Wesleyan Education Center. I prayed, "*...and Lord, help us to accept whatever happens to us today as from Your hands*". **Why** did I pray that? I don't know, it just popped into my head and I said it.

Amazingly, after the events of that day, as I lay my head on the pillow that night,... the Lord reminded me of that strange prayer. **I needed to remember what I had prayed and the powerful truth of it.** It was an amazing moment,... for me to keep remembering that prayer!

About 1:00 that afternoon, I was returning home after delivering lunch to a family whose Dad had gone to heaven. As I opened the back door, I had the thought to step back to look at the dark clouds over Greensboro. There was a little break in the clouds and I could see sky. A tiny streak of sunlight came through the hole in that dark cloud, and I thought to myself, *"Well, I'm glad the clouds aren't too thick, so Clyde can get into the airport OK."*

I've often wondered if that could have been the moment Clyde's spirit was taking it's flight to heaven, and if so, maybe he saw me standing at the back door looking up into the sky. He would also have seen the little basket in my hands, knowing I had indeed delivered lunch to the grieving family, as he had asked me to.

I went to my desk to work on the Angela Peterson Doll Museum monthly volunteer schedule. My job was to fill out the monthly calendar of volunteers who were willing to show guests around the Museum, and tell the history of the collection. Angela Peterson had moved from "up north" to live in one of the Wesleyan Arms apartments. She had given her extensive doll collection, from her travels around the world, in exchange for the apartment. She was a <u>very</u> unique lady!! Years later the Museum moved from the Wesleyan Retirement Community to a building in down town High Point.

The phone rang and Bev said, *"Ernie, have you had a call about the airplane?"* I answered no and she continued, *"I just got a call that the plane went down. They got out OK, the man told me, but the pilot's legs are burned."* When Bev said "pilot" I thought she was talking about Clyde's flight instructor. He had flown with him several times, because Clyde had just bought a different plane, and I thought perhaps he had flown with them on that day. Bev continued, *"we need to go to Cone Hospital in Greensboro to pick them up."*

We got to Cone Hospital and they took us to a small room to wait... and we waited, and I was getting VERY anxious. It seemed like a long time before a nurse and policeman came. Looking at Bev, the policeman assured her Ronnie was OK and would be going home with us. I asked, *"but what about Clyde?"*. His eyes were so sad as he looked at me saying, *"I'm so sorry, but he didn't make it."* Tears came to my eyes, but my head and my heart seemed to agree that I needed to be calm, and listen as the policeman told us what had happened, so I straightened up and listened as he explained.

The plane was losing power even though the motor was still running and Clyde **had** to find a place to land. He and Ronnie agreed and chose the intersection of Cone and Lawndale Blvds. A street sign tore a hole in the left airplane wing. As the gas ran out, it started a fire as they scooted along the pavement on the belly of the plane. Neither of the doors would open, but Ronnie was able to kick out a tiny window in the back after he prayed, *"Lord, help me."*

The manufacture representative told us later, that window was supposed to withstand 2,000 pounds of pressure. I commented, *"It was a miracle they got out."* The representative said, *"I guess that's what you could say!"*. Ronnie Sr. and the other young man were able to get out before the fire got to them.

Before I had left home, I called the school to keep Ronnie Jr. and Tammy in day care, because I was going to Greensboro to get their Dad, Ronnie Sr. and Clyde at the airport. My friend, Lucille Vernon was the receptionist and I asked her to please not tell anyone about the crash. *"Bev and I are going to pick them up at Cone Hospital and I don't want people to worry about the crash."*

Of course she called her husband, Carlis and he and Steve Denny arrived as the policeman was still talking with us. The nurse asked Carlis to come to the switchboard because the many calls were jamming their telephone lines. TV and Radio newscasters were telling about the crash with Clyde's name as the pilot.

It was after dark before Ronnie was released to go home with us. We found the parsonage yard and school parking lot full of cars, and the house FULL of people who gave us hugs and wept with us.

Kenneth was a student at Cambridge University in England, so I called one of his friends, who wisely gathered more of Ken's friends and together they told him about his Dad's plane crash. He was able to get a ticket and fly home the very next day.

It took Tuesday and Wednesday to prepare for the Thursday funeral. James Cumby, a member of our church, was our wise and loving mortician advisor. He strongly suggested that the family visitation be in the church sanctuary.

Wednesday evening, we, along with Gerald and Mary and their family started greeting people at six o'clock. We were still in the sanctuary at one o'clock in the morning hugging and being hugged by the hundreds and hundreds of people who wanted to tell us how much they loved and appreciated Clyde. The Lord miraculously gave us strength to stand those seven hours soaking up the love people expressed to us.

I was surprised to see a homeless man, humbly dressed, approaching us in the line of greeters. He told me how Clyde stopped at his "shelter" to talk with him one day urging him to come to church and accept Jesus as his Savior. He said after Clyde prayed with him, he handed him a piece of money that was so greatly appreciated. My heart was warmed by his testimony.

Our Missions Pastor, Wayne Wingfield, with a group of three or four people, broke into the line, begging to be excused by the people who were standing in the line. Pastor Wayne explained that the small group had flown into the Greensboro airport from Waxhaw, N.C. They worked for Wycliffe as Bible translators, and wanted to meet Clyde's family. Clyde had supported them financially and had flown to speak at one of their conferences, with the Rick Webb family as special music ministers. We were blessed and humbled that they had gone to so much trouble to fly to High Point and encourage us!

The next afternoon, the sanctuary and balcony were again filled for the Memorial Service. The lobby, chapel and school library were also filled, where people watched the service on closed circuit TV. People standing in the large narthex lobby made a path for us to come into the sanctuary. Clifton Wood told me years later, he was one of the people standing in the lobby, but I had no memory of seeing him.

The police told us Clyde's funeral and the procession to the Floral Garden Memorial Park was the largest in the history of High Point, even though it was an amazingly cold day. We know Clyde himself never realized the impact he had made on so many people's lives in the church, the community, the University, the state and the business community. Maybe the Lord allowed Clyde and his parents to observe that amazing February 2nd Memorial Service from their seats in heaven's balcony.

The Manager of Floral Garden Memorial Park asked us to please mark his grave with a bronze grave cover, *"so future generations will know the man buried there."* The script for the cover is a compilation of remarks from the funeral speakers: Rev. James Denny; Dr. Viola Britt; Dr. Virgil Mitchell; Dr. Douglas Covington; Dr. Melvin Gadson; Rev Raymond Shelton; and a High Point Enterprise newspaper editorial. Read again the Introduction in the front of this book, which has a copy of the grave cover.

Hundreds of cards, letters, telegrams, phone calls and personal visits to Clyde's family opened our eyes to something important. Two letters came the same day, a handwritten note from the Lieutenant Governor's office in Raleigh saying, *"North Carolina has lost one of its finest citizens...".* Another scribbled handwritten note, on yellow lined paper, told us Clyde came several times in the middle of the night when he called. He was a crippled man who cleaned trash from the downtown streets, but his bad habits got him in trouble with the law at times. I was stunned to realize Clyde was appreciated by people from the highest office in the State **and** by the street sweeper in down town High Point.

Clyde was not a gifted speaker from the pulpit, but he communicated the Gospel through his warm genuine love for people. He was not a theologian, but his administrative and leadership abilities led others to comfortably follow him and become committed Christian leaders themselves.

We received a telephone call from Senator Jesse Helms and a beautiful pot of flowers from his office the day after the crash. His help had been the reason we were able to get the HUD project for the Wesleyan Arms Retirement Community.

On the Sunday morning after the funeral Dr. Elmer Towns called from Liberty University in Lynchburg with a cheery greeting. "*The sun came up again this morning, Ernie. You can face the future with confidence, because God has much more for you to do.*"

One night my little granddaughter, Tammy, came to spend the night with me. As we prepared for bed, I suddenly felt sad and lonely for Clyde and she saw my tears. Sitting in the middle of the bed, legs crossed and her chin resting in her hands, she was so cute trying to comfort me. "*Memaw, have you thought that Pepaw is in heaven and he is happy?*" I replied, "*Oh yes, honey, I know he is happy in heaven, but I miss him so much*". Then she said, "*I like to think he has brand new skin and he's not burned anymore.*" She folded her arms as if she were holding and rocking a baby and added, "*I don't mean I think he is a **baby**, I think he has soft new skin **like** a baby.*"

Tammy taught me a great lesson that night. We can't keep sad thoughts from entering our mind, but we don't need to keep thinking sad thoughts. What we think about is our own choice. Whether we frown or smile is our own choice and whether we cry or laugh is our own choice.

Chapter 26
Growing Pains As A Widow

THERE WERE SEVERAL "cross and resurrection" cycles during the years Clyde and I raised our family of four children, each with very unique personalities. Those "cycles" continued for me, as a widow, without Clyde to help me accept them emotionally.

Clyde had been so thrilled when Kenneth chose to go to Cambridge University in England after completing a Masters of Divinity degree at Fuller Seminary in Pasadena, California. Graduating from Fuller, Ken thrilled his Dad by saying he wanted to go to England and get a PhD at Cambridge University.

A year before completing his PhD. in Church History at Cambridge, he told us he was converting to Catholicism. His Dad and I struggled in our effort to understand and graciously accept his decision, so we made a trip to England to visit him. We concluded we would dig no gulfs nor burn any bridges between us and Ken, As a side trip, Clyde rented a tiny little English car, for us to make a few days trip into Scotland which was quite enjoyable.

Arriving back at Cambridge Saturday evening, Clyde said to me, *"Ernie, don't say a thing to Ken if he takes us to a Catholic Church tomorrow morning. We want him to have no bad memories of our visit."* It was interesting that Ken decided we would enjoy the Sunday morning worship service at the Anglican Parrish Trinity Church.

Clyde Parker: Pastor; University Professor; Businessman

A few months after that trip to England, Clyde went to heaven in January, 1984. Four and half months later, Ken's friend accompanied me, on the flight, back to England for Ken's graduation in June. We felt so blessed when he got a job teaching at the University of Alabama.

I flew to Alabama and spent the New Year's Holiday with him in his bachelor's pad, eating his gourmet cooking. That weekend he shared with me that he felt God was calling him to become a Benedictine Monk at St. Andrews Priory in California.

In working through this BIG change of plans, I had to die to many things... anger, pride, embarrassment over what people would think, and the disappointment that this professional son would bury himself in a Monastery the rest of his life. He already had published a book printed by the Cambridge University Press.

I began to realize my prayers were dictating to God what He should tell Kenneth. The Lord helped me to know we can't force other people to change their minds. I became willing for God to teach me to keep loving Kenneth and leave him in God's hands, as I was learning to die to ME. I began to soften and experience the presence of the lord at a level I had not known before!

Later, I flew to St. Andrew's Priory for Ken's Investiture. For my quiet time, in my systematic Bible reading, I was at I Samuel chapters 1 and 2, where Hannah was giving her son to live in the temple for the rest of his life. I KNOW that was in God's perfect timing... it was NOT a coincidence. A thousand words from others could never have done what reading that Word from God did for me that day.

To reflect and recover from this new level of acceptance, I went for a walk up the hill behind the Priory. As if to test my resolve and compound my motherly instinct to "hang onto", the Lord allowed me to stumble into the cemetery of the Priory. Tears flooded my vision again as I reaffirmed my commitment. Finally I chose to say out loud, *"I understand, Lord, I won't even have access to his body if he dies here and that's OK".*

Annual trips to the Monastery included ceremonies at each level of Kenneth's commitment toward the vows of chastity, poverty and obedience. The gracious hospitality and loving atmosphere of the Monastery became times of personal spiritual retreat for me and I began to love those Fathers and Brothers at St. Andrews Priory.

CHAPTER 27
EVENTS AFTER CLYDE WENT TO HEAVEN

THE FIRST NIGHT, after Clyde went to heaven, I made what might have been considered a silly decision. I had the urge to sleep on Clyde's side of the bed and put my head on his pillow. That was an easy decision. The tough part came when I had to pull off that dirty pillowcase and wash away the smell of him.

Joy isn't the absence of tragedy, it is the **presence** of God and Phyllis experienced this kind of joy in a dramatic way the day before her Dad's funeral. She had gone to tidy up their Kernersville apartment just in case some out of town friends would go home with them.

As she vacuumed, she was startled to hear herself singing over the roar of the vacuum cleaner motor. She was horrified to think that someone might have heard her singing and think her terribly disrespectful to be singing so joyfully with her Dad's funeral the next day.

Just then, the title of C.S. Lewis' book <u>Surprised By Joy</u> flashed into her mind and she realized the source of her singing was from God! What was tragedy for us, was in reality, instant JOY for her Dad who was at that moment rejoicing in the presence of the Lord.

Ronnie Sr. experienced his own little miracle in a different way. Not once after the tragedy did he had a flashback or nightmare in spite of being trapped in the burning plane. His miraculous escape was also traumatic, since the small window would not accommodate his Dad's larger body and he was eyewitness to, and part of, the unsuccessful rescue attempts. We are not called to joy alone, but joy in the midst of tragedy and the resurrection power available to us now that can give us peace in the midst of tragedy.

Clyde and I had always done the Christmas shopping together, so the next December, as much as I wished for someone to take me by the hand and say, "let's go", it did not happen. So...I was jolted to reality when I realized THIS was the day we had chosen for our family Christmas party and I had not bought a thing.

By 6:00 everything was wrapped and ready and no one even suspected that everything was bought and wrapped that very afternoon. How I found presents for each person is a funny and stunning story in itself, especially the trampoline for Ronnie Jr and Tammy. Driving down the street I saw the trampoline outside a store, leaning against their sign.

After drying my tears, I went in bought it and asked them to deliver **and** set it up in Ronnie Jr. and Tammy's back yard. *"Oh, that will be impossible"*, they insisted. However, after my tearful explanation that our family celebration was that evening, they said they would try to come set it up....and they did!!! The children did not see it, until Ronnie Sr. flipped on the back yard lights at the time for them to see the present I had bought for them. They insisted I go out and jump on it with them, which I did!!!

Being alone makes one feel insignificant. It took me a couple of years not to get extremely blue on Friday evenings. Clyde and I always ate out on Fridays. A few months after Clyde went to heaven, I was filling the car with gas on a late Friday afternoon and the attendant, who was a member of our church, asked how I was doing and instantly I bust into tears. The poor guy didn't know what in the world he had said to cause such a flood. I was feeling sorry for myself. It's not just in the mind it's real!

The world feels safer when one is not alone. As long as I was looking at life from behind the shelter of Clyde... I could not possibly discover my own ability to cope with it. Change is life's way of reminding us that God made us to be flexible. We can change our dreams. God insists that we go on, not all by ourselves, but with **His help**.

Very soon after Clyde went to heaven I had to make a choice how I was going to handle a painful rejection. When someone rejects the person you have become, you will know pain that is deep, long, and sharp... pain that screams in your ears.

I received an anonymous letter in which the writer harshly condemned me for something that was untrue. I had been misunderstood. Through my tears, I decided to hibernate at home because being in public would be unbearable, not knowing who wrote the letter.

Remembering how, in the Bible story, Hezekiah spread a hurtful letter out before the Lord, I knelt by my bed and spread out that letter and asked the Lord to help me handle the hurt. I couldn't pretend the hurt wasn't there, because it was.

The Lord actually gave me the strength to get ready and go to the fellowship hall for a meeting that very night. A few days later the Lord, quite unexpectedly in answer to my earnest prayer, gave me an awareness of who wrote the letter. HE also made me aware of a kindness I could do for this elderly lady. She was not a hugger... but she hugged me and said such nice things to me, I was embarrassed.

A few weeks after Clyde went to heaven, I had a phone call asking if I would speak for a Mother/Daughter Banquet. I successfully explained I had never done anything like that and certainly did not plan to start. A few days later a lady from another church called with the same request and I made the same explanation to her, but this lady told me to pray about it and she would call back. As I hung up the phone, I burst into tears and for the first time, blamed God out loud through my tears. HE had taken Clyde to heaven, and now people were asking me to speak in public and I couldn't. I did pray about it and felt God's presence surrounding me and I knew He would be my helper. When she called back, I agreed to come.

Since that time I've had to make many more painful decisions... things I never thought I could do and didn't want to do. God was incredibly patient with my fumbling attempts to find what He wanted me to do with the rest of my life. He let me lean on Him when I had to stop for breath. I think I grew up at his insistence and in His presence.

I remember once in a moment of utter frustration, I said, *"Lord, Clyde Jr. needs his Daddy!"* Quick as a flash, He reminded me of His promise that HE would be a Father to the Fatherless. Before the day was over, He had provided incredible peace to me before I even knew about the dramatic turn of events. Clyde Jr. and Nathan Mucher were on their way back to Taylor University in Indiana and the rest of us were on a trip to Arkansas. I had tried to give Clyde Jr. more money, but he insisted he had enough. It was about 6:00 in the evening when we arrived at the Memphis airport where we were picking up Ronnie Sr.,... then continuing our trip.

The prearranged plan was for us to call the office in High Point to find out Ronnie's specific arrival time and flight number. I could see Bev's face in the phone booth registering disbelief and alternately talking and listening with a distressed look on her face. I felt it was something about Clyde Jr. and prayed that prayer reminding the Lord HE promised to be a Daddy to my children.

The facts Bev found out were that Clyde Jr had called the office in High Point saying he had two flat tires and both were beyond

Events After Clyde Went to Heaven

permanent repair and neither of the boys had enough money to buy even one tire. We found out the next day how the Lord provided for them at the Montgomery Ward store in Charleston, West Virginia.

The Office Manager was told of the plight of these college boys and she told Clyde Jr. over the phone, that she would come and let him use her personal credit card. He tried to give her his personal check to hold until he could get in touch with me to make a deposit for him, but she insisted he could just wait and send it when he had the money.

How's that for having a heavenly Daddy come to your rescue. We did send her a check for the tires, and at Christmas, I sent her some "thank you" money to buy something for herself. She forwarded that check to a ministry her sister and brother-in-law had, in New York City. She was a sister in the Lord, but she had promised to help Clyde Jr. even before she saw him or knew he was a brother in the Lord.

One of the most powerful sermons Clyde Sr. ever preached to me was only four words spoken so that only the ears of my heart heard them. Just before Clyde went to heaven I was memorizing Philippians 4:4-8 which I had written on the back of a catalog card, of a book I had discarded when I was a librarian. I left the card in Clyde's car or office, so he attached a yellow sticky note on which he had written, *"Ernie, is this yours,"* and put the card in the "home" box behind his desk.

The note was totally unnecessary, because he knew my writing, so when my eyes read the note, the question wasn't whether the card was mine. The ears of my heart heard Clyde asking me, *"Is God's peace yours, Ernie? It will be IF you meet the conditions spelled out in verses 4, 5 and 6. Rejoice **in the Lord** always...no exceptions, no conditions, ALWAYS... Be anxious about nothing, but in everything by* *prayer and supplication, with thanksgiving, let your requests be made known unto God."*

Those five verses became a powerful message from Clyde that have helped me through many bad circumstances. In fact through all the decades since Clyde went to heaven, Phil.4:4-8 has been my car license number!

One of those terrible circumstances happened two years later in 1986. I was at a missions conference in Orlando, Florida with Ardith Gallimore and Jean Neff. My parents had gone a few miles further to stay with Daddy's sister, Aunt Lily in Plant City.

Ronnie called me about midnight to tell me Mama and Daddy's house was on fire. I had moved in with them about 18 months earlier, and panicked as I mentally reviewed all the irreplaceable things that were going up in smoke. I heard myself say out loud, *"I don't want to be alone. I wish someone were here with me."* Quick as a flash, the ears of my heart heard, *"You're not alone, I'm here with you."* And suddenly, I had the feeling of being hugged. The presence of the Lord was encircling me as real as the bedcovers were covering my legs.

I reached for my Bible and began reviewing promises and claiming them. The Lord so completely satisfied my need for companionship that I didn't need to run down the hall to Jean and Ardith's room. And... miracle of miracles for an insomnia prone person, I fell into a deep sleep until morning.

Upon remembering the fire, my first thought was to rush to their room and tell them. However, the ears of my heart heard, *"so, my comfort isn't enough, you need human arms around you?"* The impression was so strong that I would be drawing attention to myself, and away from the missions focus, I decided to not share the bad news at all until we were leaving the conference, which is what I did!

November 11, 1991 Indiana Wesleyan University, in Marion, Indiana honored Clyde, a 1951 graduate, by hanging his portrait in the Hall of Heros in the Ministries Building. I was asked to speak and this is a small portion of what I said:

"... the dedicated, warm, highly respected professors of Marion College imprinted upon the minds of their students they could make a difference in their world... IF they would merge the good old American work ethic with their God-given call to be servant-ministers.... Clyde earned the title 'servant minister' in spite of all the brick and mortar accomplishments and obvious administrative ability he had.

After the funeral one of the church members said, referring to the approximately thirty-five hundred people who came to the visitation and memorial service, 'I thought I was Clyde's best friend, and now I know he was everybody's best friend.' How could such a perception happen? Clyde had trained himself to listen intently, to look the person in the eyes and then listen with the ears of his heart. This translated into genuine empathy. He would usually follow up with a written note, phone call, or personal inquiry. His trademarks were his warm letters, and telephone calls. We would jokingly say we were going to bury him with a telephone to his ear.

I was in Russia attending an International Teacher's Conference with Campus Crusade, when Ronnie Sr, had been asked to deliver the December 18, 1993 commencement address for LEAP graduates at Indiana Wesleyan University. Ken had driven from St. Louis and other family members from North Carolina to be present for a surprise Ronnie didn't know was going to happen. After his address, Dr. Barnes, the President, called Ronnie back to the podium to receive an honorary Doctorate of Business Management degree.

The family said Ronnie's talk was wonderful, in which he had reviewed his Dad's thirty-two years of accomplishments after he graduated from Marion College, now IWU. Ronnie challenged the graduate students to do the same, but his greatest challenge was for them to become best friends with the Lord and commit their lives to Him as his Dad did as a twelve year old boy. I like to think his Daddy, Clyde was cheering him on from his "grandstand" seat in heaven.

Dr. Barnes told the family it was the first time IWU had ever granted Honorary Doctorates to a father and son. Clyde had been honored with a Doctorate of Divinity in 1982 and Ronnie Sr's was an honorary Doctorate of Business Management in 1993.

Chapter 28
Remembrances by Family and Friends

Niece Anita Record Baughman, remembered the funniest story from a short visit Clyde and I made with her parents, Leo and Marietta, when Leo was a student at Bowman Gray School of Medicine in Winston Salem.

At Easter, someone had given us a baby duck, so Clyde made a little fenced area beside the parsonage side porch in Elkin. As the duck grew, Leo told us we should bring the duck to a small lake near their home in the Trailer Park in Winston Salem. Clyde tied the duck's feet together for the trip and put him in a box on the floor with Ronnie and Kenneth in the back seat of our Volkswagen.

When we arrived at Leo and Marietta's trailer home, we all went together to the little lake. Clyde commented how nice it was that the duck had not made any deposits in the box. He cut the tie from around the duck's feet and lifted him up to throw him into the lake. With his head toward the lake and his back side toward Clyde, that little duck made a HUGE deposit that landed on Clyde's white shirt!

Anita said she will never forget her Dad's hearty laughter every time he would retell family and friends how Clyde's face turned to the color of his red hair!! I don't recall where else we were going that day, but Marietta helped, as we both tried to get that stain out of Clyde's white shirt!!

I'm so glad I found these notes from a press conference Ronnie made some time in 1984:

> "... On the bright side I have memories of a Father, also my best friend, who was a legend in his own time. He was a ball of energy going at a rate of 18 to 20 hours a day, seven days a week. He had an undying faith in God and his fellow man.
>
> His greatest talent was his ability to extract the best out of those who worked around him. In 15 years he developed a church complex First Wesleyan in High Point, including nursing home and retirement apartments and the largest Day Care program in the state including a K-12 Academy program. His most recent dream for the church was to develop and sponsor a program to give unwed mothers an attractive place to live.
>
> The church complex, owned and operated by the church has recently been valued at approximately 23 million and only about 2 and half million in debt.
>
> My father was also a full professor at Winston Salem State University for the past 13 years possessing a keen burden and desire to train Minorities in the field of Teacher Education.
>
> My father was also a tremendous businessman. The programs owned by First Wesleyan in High Point are a reflection of that talent. In 1960, a dentist in Elkin, NC. sold my father three small rent houses of which he financed 100% because my father had no money. From that beginning, he was able to

develop over the next 25 years, real estate holdings including 23 nursing homes in five states.

What do I remember most about my Father? Being with him as he visited members of our church who were sick in the different hospitals in the Triad. He always knew the right things to say to encourage each one.

Fortunately, he was always planning for the expectation that he may abruptly be taken from us. He had turned his business affairs over to me, approximately two years prior to the airplane accident, giving me time to absorb the physical and mental pressure from such responsibility.

.... A gratifying experience for me this past year has been participation in the organization of a new bank in High Point, American Bank and Trust.

My mother has been a source of strength to each of the kids through this year. We have learned to take each day one at a time......

I have committed the rest of my life to fulfilling as much as possible the dreams my father had not yet accomplished."

When the two Boards of Trustees decided to merge Kernersville Wesleyan Academy with Wesleyan Christian Academy in High Point, there were many meetings in Kernersville. Some of the meetings in Kernersville were with Clarence Lambe, the banker, because he was the go-to guy for financing. Clyde and Clarence were good friends, like brothers!

Joel Farlow, Wesleyan Christian Academy Administrator, had a vivid memory of traveling one day with Clyde on Johnson Street, at the intersection of Sandy Ridge Road in Colfax. Pointing to the big tract of land, on which the farmer always grew corn, Clyde said, *"there should be a better use of **that much** land than growing corn!"*

A short time later, Joel discovered Clyde had bought that huge tract of land, and Rick Webb, who had just earned his Real Estate License, began developing the beautiful Cedar Springs residential community.

Decades later, the "farm" portion became the new site for the future Wesleyan Christian Academy campus. Joel said he would **never** have guessed the corn field they were passing that day in 1971 would indeed one day belong to High Point Wesleyan Christian Academy.

Joel continued remembering: God gifted Clyde with a unique ability to capture an opportunity and visualize what could be. Clyde came to my office one morning and simply said, *"what do you think....."* He often used that introduction to a new plan, opportunity, or concept he was considering. That day, the question was in reference to Kernersville Wesleyan Academy. *"What do you think if we merged Kernersville Wesleyan Academy with High Point Wesleyan Christian Academy and move the program to this campus?"*

Wesleyan Christian Academy in High Point, had reached its original goal to be a Pre-school – 6th grade Academy. Students could continue their Christian education enrolling at Kernersville Wesleyan Academy.

Unfortunately, the transition number never materialized. In addition, KWA's overall enrollment was declining and the future operation of the school was questionable. Merging the two schools was by far the largest undertaking Wesleyan Christian Academy in High Point had ever considered. However, it was a major opportunity to expand WCA from Preschool to 6th grade,... to a **full school** with Preschool to 12th grade in ONE YEAR.

We closed that school year in May, as a Preschool to 6th grade, and opened in the Fall offering Preschool through all High School grades. We had to use 1st Wesleyan Church Sunday School classrooms on the south end of the church for grades 7-12. Construction was immediately started on a Middle School, Gym, Dining Hall, Swimming Pool, Media Center, Offices and Classrooms.

In addition, the church board had approved the addition of a balcony in the church sanctuary. With the sanctuary under construction, as well as the new school buildings, it was obviously, a **very challenging** couple of years, but it proved to be a huge success.

For the first graduation of the expanded Wesleyan Christian Academy, Joel Farlow asked Clyde to be the Commencement speaker. *"He did an excellent job",* Joel commented. This was a perfect selection, because Clyde had been the visionary for the Pre-school, Elementary and High School.

Ed Winslow, church treasurer for many years, shared some of his vivid memories of Clyde, as his role model. *"Clyde led me to the Lord one Sunday morning during the service. He was my spiritual father and I wanted to be just like him!"* He actually was a mentor to many of the young men of the church but none of them seemed able to keep up with Clyde's pace.

He would pull out his calculator and the next thing we knew he was thinking about building another addition to the school. During a meeting, Ed remembered looking at Joel Farlow and realized they both were wondering, *"where did that come from?"* Clyde was a builder of anything that helped expand the Kingdom of the Lord.

Ed recalled going out walking with Clyde to visit the homes surrounding the church on North Centennial Street. He wanted everyone in our surrounding neighborhoods to have an invitation, by the pastor, to come to church.

One of the homes had a large German Shepherd dog outside the home. It seemed the dog didn't want visitors in the yard, so Clyde asked Ed to keep an eye on the dog! As Clyde was speaking with the home owner, the dog snuck around behind them and started pulling on Ed's backside! Ed whacked him pretty hard on his nose with the clipboard he had in his hand. Clyde nor Ed any recollection of that neighbor ever visiting the church!

Ed remembered when Clyde turned fifty, the church staff, pastors and families decided to have a fun birthday party at the rustic Hillbilly Hideaway Restaurant tucked into a cleared forest. Decorated with black balloons, everyone was having great fun teasing him about getting old! Clyde had let the group know the treat was on him, as a "thank you", for being such great helpers at the church.

When it came time to pay, the owner told Clyde he would not accept his check in payment since he had been cheated by some Christians from time to time. The owner was giving him a hard time in front of everyone, and Clyde was acting as if he were very embarrassed.

Ed recalled how angry the group was feeling toward the owner for treating Clyde that way. He even had us digging into our wallets trying to come up with some cash to help pay for the food. All of a sudden, Clyde and the owner started laughing heartily, and we realized they had pulled a big joke on us. The owner and Clyde had planned it all the time.... as he accepted Clyde's check.

Victory Mountain Youth Camp tucked into a hilly, heavily forested area near Sophia, has accomplished so much for Christ's Kingdom through the decades. The wisdom of Clyde Parker, James Denny and the Board of Trustees in the North Carolina East District of the Wesleyan Churches, made the decision to build the camp primarily for children and teenagers.

A beautiful lake was developed while the buildings were being built. Most camps at that time were being built for adults. Ed shared he has read all the founding documents and marvels at how these men and women were used by the Lord to create such a GREAT place, for adults as well as for children.

I found a letter, tucked away in one of the "history boxes", that Ed wrote to me in 1984 ten months after Clyde went to heaven. My eyes leaked tears, reading again Ed's description of Clyde's untiring work as pastor of 1st Wesleyan Church. Some of his letter has already been written in previous chapters, but this is a portion of what Ed wrote:

".... For a young Christian like myself to get the great opportunity to have a spiritual father like Clyde was a gift from God.... I remember going to my great grandmother's funeral at the Welch Methodist Church in Archdale and it really touched my heart that Clyde would care enough about me to come to her funeral. As busy as he was, Clyde was willing to catch up with his own work later and see after my needs at that time.... Soon after that I got involved with the Bus Ministry and many other ministries too.... My mother and Carolyn thought I was overdoing it, but I saw Clyde working so hard trying to get the needs of his Jerusalem taken care of that I really got burdened for Clyde... God gave me a dose of Clyde's spirit that I will always carry with me. He was a man who loved people and would do anything he could to help out his fellowman.... I remember going out with Clyde one day over on the street behind the Wesleyan Arms. I always got the biggest kick out of watching him handle dogs. He had a healthy respect for dogs–especially big dogs. We had two experiences that day that I'll never forget. I believe Clyde was touched by the fact we

visited a lady who said she had lived there for over ten years and no church had ever visited her except us. She meant it as a compliment, but Clyde was thinking that she lived that close to us and even we had let her down. He mentioned it more than once before we got back to the church. On that same street we met a lady just leaving her house. Clyde told her who we were but she said she had to rush to the hospital. Her husband had just had an accident. Clyde quickly asked he if he could pray for her and her husband and she seemed so grateful. After he prayed, Clyde gave her a hug. He actually gave that stranger a hug.... Clyde was truly a good Samaritan!... I hope we can have a book written about Clyde's life. I want my kids to be able to know about great men of faith like Clyde.... Clyde Parker is one of the great saints of our age. If people really knew Clyde like I knew Clyde and were able to see just how true he really was to his calling, I think that would motivate them to want a deeper relationship to God and give them a greater burden for God's work..... Well, it's 4:00 a.m. and I'm getting sleepy. I've been meaning to write you this letter for ten months and I just felt that tonight was the night. God bless you and your family. Love, Ed Winslow

Iris Mitchell, had been a faithful member of High Point First Wesleyan Church for decades. She gave me a great summary of her memory of Clyde through his 18 years of ministry at 1st Wesleyan Church. This was her last paragraph: *"... He was a remarkable godly man. He was at work all the time whether it was local, district or nationally. We were all greatly blessed to have him as pastor, builder, and friend. I am so thankful to have benefitted from his many endeavors."* What makes Iris' comments even more impressive, is the fact that in 2022, when she wrote this, she was 98 years old!!

Remembrances by Family and Friends

****

Eddie Williams shared how stunned he was one day, decades ago when looking through Clyde's car window, he saw a telephone cradled between the two front seats. Clyde had invested in the phone so he could make calls while away from the office or driving from school, so he didn't waste any minutes. During the late 1970s, early 1980s, wireless telephones were so rare, lots of times people would gape at Clyde talking on a telephone **in his car!!**

The car trunk housed the technical parts with wires running from the trunk under the car and up to the telephone between the two front seats. Since he usually put nearly 50,000 miles a year on a car, he traded cars almost every year. However, he was willing to invest in the technical process of taking the phone out and putting it into the new car each year.

When he needed to make a call, he would pick up the telephone and see if anyone else was using their wireless phone. If the phone was open he would say, *"This is 4525, would you please ring....."* Each of the telephone operators became one of his friends, and would sometimes carry on conversations with him.

I remember on long trips, to keep from dropping off to sleep, I would pick up the telephone and listen to conversations, and they didn't realize I was listening to them. Car telephones were very public, so you never had private conversations, because you never knew who was listening.

Chapter 29
Lessons From Living Life

One day by Providential design I found a way to describe the incredible peace God gave me during the months and years after Clyde went to heaven. I went to Myrtle Beach with Ronnie Sr. and Steve Denny to survey damage after Hurricane Diana.

Waiting for the boys at one of the rescue offices, I talked with one of the brave volunteers who drove a rescue vehicle all during the height of the storm, taking people to places of safety. He was a ruddy macho outdoorsman and I listened intently, as he described what he said was the most frightening experience of his whole life. There was deafening noise, flying debris and rain so thick he felt he was under water at times.

Twice during the day, he said he experienced the eye of the hurricane as the storm meandered overland. He described how all of a sudden the sky was blue all the way up. There was no wind. There was no rain and the sea gulls even ventured out. The noise was still there and he could see the storm swirling out there all around him, but it wasn't touching him. He could see the effects, but he couldn't feel it.

As he talked, I felt a tingle of excitement. The "eye of the hurricane" is a proven fact of natural science that we all accept, even though we don't quite understand it.

At last I had found a way to describe what I had experienced since Clyde went to heaven. The facts were not changed. Clyde was no longer with me. My earthly prop was gone and some frustrating circumstances kept intensifying into terrible personal storms. It is then I scramble to my place of peace. The song says, "*There is a place of quiet peace, near to the heart of God.... Hold us, who wait before Thee, near to the heart of God.*"

Chapter 30
Pastor James Denny's 1984 Memorial Day Message

Sermon Excerpts: "Let the Church Roll On"... Text: Zechariah 4: 6... Given at First Wesleyan Church Homecoming and Memorial Day Service, High Point, North Carolina... Sept. 23, 1984... Dedicated to Dr. Clyde A. Parker's Memory by Senior Pastor Rev. James L Denny...

The year 1984 has been a year thus far we shall never forget here at First Wesleyan Church! In the afternoon of January 30, 1984, I received a phone call from a Major in the High Police Department asking me if I would be in my office for a few minutes. I said, *"Yes,"*... and the officer said, *"We will be there in just a few minutes; we have a message for you."*

He and Detective Jim Tobin, who is a member of the church, came to my office and gave me the shocking and heart-breaking news that Dr. Clyde Parker, our Senior Pastor, my dear friend of 35 years, had been killed in the forced landing of his airplane on Cone Boulevard in Greensboro. What a terrible shock that was to our church and to our whole campus.

Following Dr. Parker's death, a television reporter asked me, *"What will happen to this place now?"* And I answered, *"It is going to go on! It is the Lord's Work! We have suffered a great loss, and we will miss Dr. Parker's vision and leadership very much; but it is going to go on!"*

In 1968 First Wesleyan Church needed an Associate Pastor and God had His man waiting and ready. He was a man of unusual ability in many areas, and he was, without doubt, God's Man for the hour. This man was born in high gear... a man with a very high level of energy and a man with a God-given vision as well as a God-given ability to establish the extensive outreach ministries that are now a part of this church.

That man, as you know, was the late Dr. Clyde A. Parker, Sr., whom God, for reasons known only to Himself, saw fit to take to heaven last January 30. (As I think about him today, I wonder what he is trying to build in heaven.)

Soon there was the Wesleyan Education Center; then the Wesleyan Arms Retirement Center; then the Transportation Ministry; then the Multi-Media Ministry; then the First Wesleyan Endowment Fund Ministry; then the Counseling Ministry; and then the Wesleyan Institute of Music and Arts, and the co-operative relationship with John Wesley College,... and the church was rolling on!

Since the Fall of 1949, on the streets of Marion, Indiana, when I walked up and introduced myself to Clyde and Ernie Parker, we have been life-long friends and associates. How could I turn him down when in 1972 he came down to Randleman, North Carolina, and asked me to come and administer the newly chartered Retirement Center? I probably would have turned him down, but God said, *"That is where I want you!"* So we began to serve together as Pastors of this church and complex.

It still seems unbelievable that Dr. Parker is gone, but we say today, *"May God bless his memory; and may God help us to accept the challenge and to see to it by the* help *of God, that* **The Church Rolls On Until Jesus Comes!"**

CPSIA information can be obtained
at www.ICGtesting.com
Printed in the USA
JSHW020049211222
35248JS00004B/6

9 781662 863967